TALES
OF
A
NORFOLK CHEF

by
Colin Rushmore

A donation from the proceeds of this book
will go to the Phoebe Ward Cerebral Palsy Fund.

Copyright

Published by Colin Rushmore, Rushmore's Restaurant, 14 High Street, Heacham, Norfolk PE31 7ER.

© Copyright Colin Rushmore 2003.
The rights of Colin Rushmore to be identified as sole author of this book.

© Copyright of photographs, Colin Rushmore, Eastern Daily Press 2003.

Cover photograph by John Hocknell Eastern Daily Press

Printed by Witley Press Hunstanton Norfolk

ISBN 0-9546436-0-7

Contents

Acknowledgements

There is a saying that behind every successful man there is a good woman, it is very true in my case, Kathy my wife or Mrs R as she is often known.
For this and many other reasons I would like to dedicate this book to her.

My thanks go to Pat and Malcolm. Without their patience, perseverance and support I would have given up writing the book many months ago.

Also a very special thank you to Chris Bishop and John Hocknell from the Eastern Daily Press for their understanding and help.

To the staff of Rushmore's, who over the last six months have put up with me constantly going on about the book, thanks.

At Rushmore's we source the finest of local meat, game and fish, many of these have been used in the recipes in this book. So it is to Scoles of Dersingham and Alan Howard of Heacham who both supply the restaurant with its meat and game and also to Coles of King's Lynn, for the freshest of fish; a big thank you.

Last but not least, I wish to thank my customers, for without them there would be no Rushmore's Restaurant.

About the Author

Born in 1944 as the war was coming to an end, it was a hard time to grow up, but on the other hand I would not have had it any other way. In those days you could leave your house door unlocked, and most people knew all the residents that lived in the street.

Those were the days before the television ruled the living room. We listened to the steam radio, and I remember having to go and pick up the batteries from a man who, for sixpence, would charge them up for you.

It was in the days when you could stay out all day, and nobody would be sent looking for you. It was when summer days lasted forever.

Mother and father worked long hours, so my sister and I always stayed at my grandmother's house before being collected by mother on her way home. My childhood was a very special and happy time and now, on looking back, I realise that my inspiration for cooking came from the time that I spent in my grandmother's company.

Grandmother was an excellent cook and was always baking cakes, or roasting game that had been shot by my grandfather. There seemed to always be hares and rabbits in the larder waiting to be cooked and I believe that being brought up as a young boy in this environment made a lasting impression on me.

Christmas time was not as it is today. There was no nipping down to the supermarket to get supplies for that special day.

Weeks of preparation were required, and as Christmas Day grew closer there were days of baking to be sorted out so that we could enjoy mince pies and the unforgettable sherry trifle.

When I left school my love for food started me on the first steps of the ladder of cooking. The Dukes Head, in the Market Place in King's Lynn, was my first port of call. This was in the very early 60's. These were very happy times as for the first time I was learning the trade that was to see me through the next forty plus years.

I was very proud to have been offered work with a great chef Mr Frank Cotton. To a young commis chef Frank Cotton was a friend, and a master, all rolled into one. He was my mentor.

After three years I was offered a second chefs position at the four star Manor Hotel set in the countryside at Ingoldisthorpe in Norfolk. Anybody that was anybody at the time dined at the Manor. It had been at one time the manor house of the village and had also been the country house of a certain lady who, on her 100th birthday, was visited by six heads of state that were staying at Sandringham.

As a young second chef it was up to me to prove that I could cook. Head chefs seemed to come and go, and often there were weeks that I was left in charge of the hotel's kitchens. I suppose that the owners got fed up with these chefs coming and going and at the tender age of twenty two I was given the chance to take over the Manor's kitchens as head chef.

I was at the Manor for a number of years and as head chef I started to build up a reputation for fine food. Then as the hotel had just been sold I thought it was time to move on.

It was the Black Horse Inn at another Norfolk village, called Castle Rising, which became home to me for the next ten years.

The Black horse in those days was an old fashioned village Inn. It served freshly cooked food sourced from local suppliers and was only a few miles from the Sandringham Estate. I can honestly say that, in the ten years that I worked there, I could count on one hand the times that the restaurant was not full for lunch and dinner.

As I have said the Black Horse was my home for ten years but even after all those years it was once again time to find pastures new.

The Riverside Restaurant was my next restaurant. Maybe because of my long stint at the Black Horse, I only worked there for just a year. It was a new restaurant and was set up in bistro style, which was not what I was used to.

It was at this time in my life that I thought it was right to start and open my own restaurant. In my search for a restaurant, I had a chance meeting with my old friend John Brundle, father of Martin Brundle the racing driver. John said that he would be pleased to pop a few bob into the honey pot and to cut the story short, restaurant La Casa was born.

La Casa was my first restaurant. It was a very busy place in the 1980's and I often arrived home in the early hours of the morning. Then with a couple of hours sleep, I was back at the restaurant to start it all over again. In the following years I bought John out and after getting a contract to supply 1000 meals a week for the Sandringham Estate, I then decided to sell La Casa and put my heart and soul into the outside catering that was to be called Colin Rushmore Cuisine.

The outside catering lasted for 12 years, often working throughout the night so to complete functions. The food that we produced was responsible for taking us into many of the finest houses in Norfolk including the Royal House at Sandringham.

With my mind made up I felt that the outside catering would have to be slowed down. This took over a year due to all the advanced bookings that we had. Once again a chance meeting with a customer that used La Casa, decided my new direction. He had, with two partners, just brought a run down hotel by the coast and offered me the position of general manager.

For the first time I was not in my favourite terrain of the kitchen. But not for long and it was a good thing that I had a habit of keeping a set of chef's whites and my trusty knives in the boot of my car.

Normally if the chef fails to turn up for duty, then all hell breaks loose. That's why most chefs get away with murder, but not in this case and it did not take long to prove it.

My management days lasted for five years, the chef whites and knives came out of the boot on many occasions and in a way I was pleased that they did. The love and passion to return to being a chef was becoming stronger each day. I knew that there was a restaurant that had been closed down. It was a pity that a lovely restaurant in a quaint village of Heacham in Norfolk was empty. But not for long, in October 2001 Rushmore's restaurant was born. I was back in my kitchen cooking local meat and fish; serving once again to customers that love and enjoy fine food.

TERRINES AND PATES

I suppose that over the many years that I have been making pates, I could have filled the average village hall with the stuff.

When I started out in the sixties I watched the old chef produce a terrine of duck liver pate. After the first cooking, all the ingredients were passed through a hand-operated mincer that was screwed to the worktop in the kitchen. It was a very messy operation as the warm juices often overflowed the small hopper on the top of the mincer.

Once the pate was in the form of a thick liquid, chef would then add a small amount of brandy. Trying a little first to see if it was up to standard, before slowly stirring it in to add that little bit of what ever, that chef had convinced himself the brandy did to the pate.

The next job was to find the pudding bowls. These were lined out with uncooked streaky bacon and after chef had correctly seasoned the pate, this was gently spooned into the bowls, making sure that the bacon was held in place. After this performance had been completed the second cooking had to take place. The bowls were placed in a large tray of water; a ring of greased paper was cut to size and gently laid on top of each bowl. This was to stop the heat of the oven burning the pate. Slowly the tray would be slid into a medium hot oven and cooked for about one hour.

Once this had been achieved, the tray was removed from the oven and the bowls of duck pate were allowed to cool completely before they were stored in the fridge, ready for service.

A lot of time and effort, for what you may say, but take a sharp knife and slice yourself a wedge of terrine of duck pate, add a little tawny port sauce, or the classic Cumberland sauce and some freshly toasted bread. Then you will realise that time and effort is an important part of this dish and you have on your plate pate of a quality that you will be very hard pushed to buy from a shop.

Chicken Liver Pate with Cumberland Sauce

This is a simple way of making a chicken liver pate. Thank goodness that over the years some clever person has invented the electric blender. This saves so much time compared with popping spoonfuls of hot livers into a small hopper and then the coordination of turning the handle at the same time.

To start with you will require 2lb of fresh chicken livers, one medium size onion, two or three slices of back bacon, a bay leaf or two, and around 1lb of butter or a very good quality margarine, salt and pepper for the seasoning and that is basically all you need to make this simple pate.

Find yourself a thick- bottomed saucepan of a good size; pop in the butter, but save back a small amount for sealing the pate once it is cold and set. Gently melt the butter over the heat; you mustn't let it burn so keep an eye on it. Next skin and chop fine the onion and add to the butter. Dice the bacon and add this to the pan, and last but not least add the chicken livers and bay leaves.

Now it's wooden spoon time. Slowly turn up the heat and start stirring. The idea is to cook the ingredients in the pan over the heat with out burning them. The chicken livers will require cooking completely as this recipe will not need a second cooking stage.

When the chicken livers are completely cooked and only then, pour the mixture, including all the juices but less the bay leaves, into the blender and turn it on to produce a lump free liquid. This may take two or three minutes to perfect. The pate is now ready to be seasoned to your taste. Add salt and pepper slowly and mix well in, taste, season and taste, in that order. You cannot remove the seasoning if you have over done it, so take your time and add a little at a time. All you need now is to find a pudding bowl and spoon it into it. Allow it to cool before melting the butter you saved and pour this over the pate to form a seal. I would normally serve this chicken liver pate with a spicy sauce and the classical Cumberland sauce is the one I prefer.

Cumberland Sauce

To make the Cumberland sauce you will require the grated rind and juice of one nice sized orange, and also the grated rind and the juice of a lemon, a good half-full cup of port, a little splash of red wine vinegar, four to five ounces of redcurrant jelly, and just the hint of salt.

Put a splash of water in a small saucepan and add the grated orange and lemon rinds and simmer gently for a few minutes. Next pop in the port, also the vinegar and redcurrant jelly, stirring all the time until the jelly melts. Then add the juices of the fruits, and a pinch of salt. Stir well over a low heat, to incorporate all the flavours, for five minutes. You can use it as a warm sauce or allow it to go cold and serve with the terrine of chicken livers.

ASPARAGUS

In June the first asparagus appears. As it only has a short season we, at the restaurant, recommend it to our customers as  we offer them the menu. Fresh English asparagus, grown just a few miles up the road from us, is like tasting early summer on a plate; freshly cut in the early morning and delivered to the restaurant ready for lunch service.

It is only when the customers' order for asparagus arrives in the kitchen that we will prepare and cook it. We start by trimming off the hard white end of the stalk with a sharp knife. On the stove I would have a saucepan that has a few inches of boiling water in it that has been slightly salted. Over the years I have tried all ways of cooking asparagus and this is the one that I prefer.

With the portion of asparagus lightly tied with string, I place it gently into the boiling water. The young tender asparagus will only take a few minutes to cook, and you can test to see if it's ready by using the tip of a sharp knife. If it just goes through the stalk end, but still feels firm then your asparagus is ready.

Gently lift it out with a spatula and allow it to drain. Take a few seconds to absorb the scent given off by freshly cooked asparagus. It makes you want to eat it yourself. All we need now is a nice creamy rich sauce, but not so overpowering that it takes away the flavours of what you are eating.

Asparagus with Hollandaise Sauce

With your asparagus all prepared and ready to be cooked, it's time to make this classic sauce called Hollandaise. It's a light sauce that goes well with other dishes, including salmon or sea bass. Come to think about it, it goes with any food that requires a little light sauce, which will not upset the delicate balance of the product. So to make the hollandaise sauce....

Hollandaise Sauce

To make a hollandaise sauce I would normally use three good size egg yolks, a pinch of salt, one tbsp of white wine vinegar, a small squeeze of lemon juice and 6oz of butter. Forget all that messing about stirring the sauce over a double boiler and get out the food processor. Place the egg yolks into the food processor with the pinch of salt.

In a small saucepan heat the wine vinegar and lemon juice and reduce this by half, next pop your butter in another small saucepan and bring up to heat, but don't let it burn. Switch the processor, that contains the egg yolks, on to high speed, and pour in the slightly warm vinegar. Then slowly add the melted butter. This must be done with a little more care and you can give the sauce a twist or two of black pepper if you feel it requires it.

If you make the hollandaise in advance, just switch the processor back on for a few seconds and add a few drops of boiling water if the sauce becomes too thick. A perfect sauce for your samphire or fish, not forgetting asparagus.

SAMPHIRE

Only the locals ate samphire, until a few years ago. Now it's served in all of the best London restaurants. The weather slightly depicts the season, but we are normally ready to start cooking the first of the samphire in early June.

At home we always look forward to the arrival of the samphire man. It seems that he has been coming round every year and he must be well into his eighties, "Samphire, Samphire." he calls at the top of his voice, and as you round the corner you will see him standing with his horse-drawn trailer loaded up with freshly picked samphire. I suppose by now the horse, which has been his constant companion, could do the round on its own.

I have never collected samphire from the mud flats myself but I would think that it's a bit of a messy job. The thought of paddling in mud at low tide, in my chef's gear to gather samphire for that evening's service, really is taking the job a tad too far. Best left to those that does it for a living, and that old saying every man to his own.

Samphire they say is poor man's asparagus, for some it may be, but if you look on any good restaurant menu, you will see it being served with hollandaise sauce or as a garnish to wild sea bass. However I believe that, like many foods sourced from the wild, it requires simple cooking and not much else added to enjoy its true flavours.

Samphire with Warm Butter

When the samphire arrives I normally put it into a sink that is filled with water and give it a good wash. Once this has been done you will require the aid of a strong pair of scissors. These are to remove the roots of the samphire. After this task has been achieved it's time for another wash in cold water just to make sure that none of the mud flats will be served up with your dish.

To cook the samphire is a simple operation. Have a good-sized saucepan of boiling water on the stove. This must contain sufficient water to cover the samphire once it has been added. Do not add any salt to the water, as you will find that the cooked samphire will not require it.

Once the water is boiling put in the samphire in one go, and gently give it a stir to make sure that it's all under water. How long will it take to cook? The answer to that is as long as it takes. It must be kept simmering and I would normally lift a bit out to try after ten minutes.

The test, to see if it's cooked, is very simple. For those with tender hands I suggest that you dip your piece of samphire in a bowl of cold water just to cool it down and so you can handle it with out burning your fingers. Now hold the root end between your fingers and with your other hand try to remove the green flesh. If it slides easily away leaving a thin stick like thing in your fingers then your samphire is cooked. If not continue the cooking for a few more minutes and test again.

All that is required once the samphire is ready is to drain it and place in a large bowl. To create the simple butter sauce, gently melt the amount of butter that you think you will need in a small saucepan, add a good squeeze of lemon juice and a few turns of freshly milled black pepper, and pour it over the warm samphire.

Now the fun begins. To eat your samphire you hold the root end between your fingers, then gently dip it in the butter sauce, and this is the hard bit, with the samphire now covered in a oily butter sauce its a coordinated movement of the wrist that pops the samphire in to your mouth. Get this action wrong, and well look at you! Never mind, it must beat paddling about up to your eyes in mud, on a wet day, collecting samphire.

STRAWBERRIES

One of the things that I try to do at Rushmore's Restaurant is to offer a selection of dishes that are in season. We have cooked and served what seem endless bundles of local asparagus all served up with a hollandaise, or warm butter sauce. You could say it's the taste of summer on a plate.

Once the English asparagus season comes to an end, we are turning to another local dish and that is Norfolk samphire. It would be more than silly of me to tell a Norfolk person how to cook samphire. It would be like telling Granny how to suck eggs. But if there are any grannies out there that have forgotten, then I am at the Restaurant most days and I would be only too pleased to help.

Strawberries, did you say strawberries? What a treat we are offered in this part of Norfolk. Fresh from the straw lined fields to us, and for less than most fruits pound for pound.

What to do with strawberries, if they make it home? That is if little fingers don't help themselves so as a word of warning leave them alone, Dad.

It was the Beatles that sang "Strawberry fields, let me take you down, strawberry fields forever." Well all I can say is that I prefer my strawberries in a punnet.

I still have a painful memory of picking them in the early hours of the morning and the agony of the so-called walk that is only experienced by first time pickers and is for some reason called the strawberry walk.

As a young child I would go picking with my grandmother, as this would help her with a little extra money that she would put aside to buy little things for Christmas: tins of biscuits, or the odd tin of salmon. All these treats would be locked away in the old Welsh dresser of which she was the sole key holder.

If you have never tasted a freshly pulled strawberry, still dripping with the morning dew, then all I can say is you have never lived.

Warm Norfolk Strawberries with Ice Cream!

Strawberries, as we all know, can only be served in one way and that's simply with fresh whipped fresh cream. Perfection in a dish if ever there was one, served up with a nice glass of chilled white wine. You don't need to look in any cookery books for that recipe. But if you have a glut of fresh strawberries and want to try something different then this is as good as it gets.

Search and find a medium size saucepan, place it over a low heat. To the pan you add a good knob of butter, as they say the size of two large walnuts. Gently let this melt without letting it brown.

To this you add the same two walnuts worth of brown sugar. The sugar must be mixed with butter. It often helps if you draw the pan off the heat. As soon as you have a smooth sugar paste return the pan to the heat and add half a cup of warm water. Control the heat and you will finish up with syrup. In this syrup you may be tempted to put a shot of whisky; that's up to you, it works well without it.

Now for the strawberries, these will have been hulled and washed and all you do is gently pop them into the warm syrup, leave on a gentle heat for a minute. This gives you time to get out the ice cream. After you have put your ice cream in the dishes, it's time to spoon the warm strawberries over - and then you have Warm Norfolk strawberries with ice cream! Pop a Beatles record on the record player. Strawberry Fields Forever.... what else?

SOUPS

On a cold winter night, a freshly made soup served with crusty bread is a treat to remember. You can make a good soup out of almost anything and, as a young commis chef, at the hotel in the early sixties, it was my job to produce two large saucepans of one white and one brown soup before chef arrived on duty at 9.30.

Each pan held many gallons of freshly made soup and each was made in the traditional way starting with a roux. The correct amount of margarine was placed in a pan and melted; then the flour was added and stirred well in to form what is called a roux. Once this was ready you added the stock from the large stockpot that was always simmering on the end of the stove, slowly stirring to take out any lumps. The soup, if it was supposed to be cream of chicken, had lots of chicken bones added to obtain flavour. It was now left on a low heat for a good hour or so before it was pushed through a giant strainer.

This strainer had two wooden rollers attached to a long handle and as you pulled and pushed on the handle the soup would be forced through the fine meshed strainer into another pot. Then you would have to carry the pot back to the stove and add fresh cream plus salt and pepper to season.

Preparation of these soups was only part of my job. If I was on the breakfast shift, it had to be fitted in between, cooking seventy full English breakfasts, starting off the roasts for lunch, trying to read chef's little notes that he had left me and preparing scrambled egg on toast for thirty staff breakfasts. This was for all those that had been on duty from six in the morning, and with a lunch and dinner shift still to look forward to I was looking forward to my day off.

BROWN SHRIMPS

The fact is I love the taste of brown shrimps. Anybody that has tasted them will fall in love with them as well. The little shrimps that are caught in the Wash are the sweetest of all.

We, at the restaurant, have tried all sorts of ways of serving them; potted in a lightly flavoured mace butter, served with warm toast or deep fried in a tempura batter served with a very light lobster sauce. However the best way and the one that sells the most is a simple little dish of brown shrimp fishcakes served with a lime butter sauce.

When I was aged around ten years old I use to visit my grandmother who would peel shrimps for a living. As I remember it there was a room of probably twenty ladies, sitting at tables that were piled high with brown shrimps. These ladies were paid for every pound that they peeled. The floor was just a mass of shrimp shells that the plant owner would sweep into a pile that would be disposed of.

Looking back, what a waste! The shells could have been made into a beautiful soup, or a fresh shrimp sauce that would have knocked your boots off.

In the wintertime I would be sent round to the bakers, that was only a few yards from the shrimp factory, for twenty odd bread rolls. As you arrived at the bakers you could warm your hands on the wall of the bake house. The heat from the ovens warmed the outside wall and you would often see old men warming their hands in the frosty weather.

On arriving back with the warm rolls, that would each cost 1p in old money, they would be filled with freshly peeled shrimps. Freshly baked bread and freshly peeled brown shrimps is food for the gods; if you have tasted better then good luck to you.

Brown Shrimp Fishcake

Here is a very simple dish to prepare. For one pound of brown shrimps you will require one pound of mashed potato that has been well seasoned.

Once the potato is cold add the peeled brown shrimps and mix well. You can add a little chopped parsley if you have some. The next thing to do is shape the fishcakes, and dip them in freshly made breadcrumbs. It is up to you if you prefer two small ones or just one large fishcake.

Remember we use them as a starter, but if required they can be as a main course, served with a nice fresh salad. It takes only a few minutes in a deep fat pan to fry these fishcakes.

All it requires to perfect the taste of these is to serve with a little warm butter to which some chopped lime has been added. Far from the days of freshly baked bread filled with brown shrimps, but just as good.

DUCKS

It's a long time ago since I was a commis chef. I was at the time working with a man I can only describe as a friend, but more than that he was my mentor. He gave me my inspiration in those early days and without his help and friendship I would not be the chef that I am today.

Chef Frank Cotton, chef de cuisine, was his name. All the staff, in the seventy-roomed four-star hotel, thought he was a god and at that time I was one of four commis chefs that worked under him. Yes, Frank Cotton was god, a father, and a friend, respected in his domain, and thank goodness that he spotted a glimmer of talent in a young chef, and helped me to go on to greater things. I have tried to follow in the footsteps of a man I respected. There are many stories that I could write about him. In fact that's probably another chapter, or maybe another book.. I was, as they say, in the right place at the right time.

It was in the early 1960's that I started at the hotel. Frank was in charge of the kitchens, and I came into that environment as a commis chef. I remember seeing cucumbers, tomatoes, and lettuces at Christmas time; at home we only saw these in the summer months.

One of the things that the four commis chefs did as a regular thing was to have a race. We placed four plucked fresh ducks on a chopping board; on your marks, ready, go. The aim of the race was to see how fast one could chop off the heads and remove the insides from the four ducks and have them ready for the oven. I am glad to say that I held the record for that, under thirty seconds, not bad for an old Norfolk boy!

We cooked the ducks in those days in an old coal-fired oven that was kept up to maximum heat by a kitchen porter. I must say woe betide him if the temperature fell below what chef considered to be a fair working heat. It was at that time I felt sorry for the porter as he and his little poker tried, often in vain, to revive the fire that he had neglected.

The ducks, depending on their size, were cut into four or five portions and served with a fresh orange sauce that was called some silly French thing in those days. But often, to our amazement, chef would carve the whole duck off the bone and send it through to the restaurant for the headwaiter to do his special thing with.

It was months later, on a visit into the restaurant, that I found this thing that you could say came from the dungeons. In fact it was called a duck press. It appears that after the duck had left the kitchen the bones of the duck were placed in this press and all the juices were squeezed out, then heated on a flambé lamp and from this a rich sauce was made to pour over the duck. Sadly these days of the front man have long gone, along with his stiff collars and tails. I, for one, am grateful to have started work in the days when he, the headwaiter, was still respected and king of his restaurant.

Roasted Duck with Orange Sauce

Place the duck in a good roasting tray breast side up. I normally put a small amount of oil on the duck, but beware, as the bird will give off so much fat that it may at times need to be drained off. Roasting time is approx one and a half hours for a good size Norfolk duck that is to be cooked well done rather than slightly under cooked and pink.

As the duck is cooking, it's time to prepare the simple orange sauce to go with this bootifull flavoured meat. The sweetness of the orange goes very well with this dish in fact it's a great classic dish still served in my restaurant today.

To make the sauce I cheat a little. I obtain a bottle of fresh orange juice and bring this to the boil in a small saucepan. To this I add sliced orange rind and when the juice has been simmering for a few minutes, I thicken this with a drop of corn flour that has been mixed with water. And there you have it a nice orange sauce ready to pour over the sliced duck.

To present the dish, slice the duck into four, that's two breast portions and two legs. Place in the centre of a good size plate and pour over the hot orange sauce. You can, if you wish, add a few fresh slices of orange to decorate the plate.... a real classic duck in orange sauce.

RABBITS

I can still remember the sight of my grandmother as she opened the old log fired oven door to reveal a roasting pan that contained a rabbit that had been slowly cooking in cider. There never seemed to be a shortage of rabbits for the pot as my grandfather owned a 12 bore shotgun, and I can recall that rabbit was served at least once a week in her house.

In those days it seemed that the main meal of the day was always served at lunch times followed by a smaller meal of simpler food at what was called tea time.

Often I would be sent out with grandfather to walk with him on his rabbit hunting trips. I suppose this was to get me out from under my grandmother's feet. We would normally set out just as the sun was starting to go down; this seemed to be the best time according to grandfather as the rabbits would be starting to come out of the burrows to feed.

Grandfather had lots of rules that I, as a young lad, had to remember and obey. Number one was I always had to walk behind him, at least five paces. Number two; I was taught how to walk with out making a noise. This I found difficult to say the least, and often felt the old flat cap, that he wore, across the back of my neck.

More often than not, just at the vital moment, when he was about to fire, I unfortunately moved and crack, I had just stood on a dry old stick. Not only did grandfather hear the noise but so did every rabbit within miles. After a few well-deserved whacks with his cap I soon learnt to stand very still. There was a list of about ten dos and don'ts, eleven if you add the one that it was my job to go and retrieve the rabbit.

If we had had a good shoot then we often walked as far as the village pub. Grandfather would say "Hold you here, boy. I wont be long." He was always true to his word and after a few minutes he would appear with a bottle of fizzy lemonade and a packet of crisps, which, once opened, you had the pleasure of finding the little blue salt bag and salting your crisps. Grandfather never came out of the pub with the same amount of rabbits that he went in with. I suppose they had paid for his beer and my lemonade and crisps.

As we strolled along the lane leading up to the house, grandfather put his hand on my shoulder and said "One more rule, boy. If you want to come rabbiting with me agin, don't tell your grandmother about us stopping off at the old Maids Head." Remembering that whenever you saw grandfather he was always wearing his old flat cap, and the pain of it coming in contact with the back of my neck, of course I never did say a word.

Slow Cooked Rabbit
in a Cider Sauce with Shallots

If you are choosing a rabbit for the pot from a butcher's look for one that has very little damage from shooting. Also pick a rabbit that has white flesh. I always wash it in a little salted water and dry with a clean cloth.

Prepare the rabbit by removing the back legs, then the saddle and lastly the basket and front legs. This can be done with a large knife or a cleaver. Once you have your portions of rabbit dust them in a little flour. Next find a good thick-bottomed saucepan, into this pour a little oil, and place the pan on a medium heat.

When the oil is hot add your rabbit portions. It's always best to use a chef's fork to turn the rabbit so it browns on both sides. When the rabbit meat is nicely sealed, add three or four bay leaves, and a large onion that has been chopped. This will add flavour. Pour yourself a glass of cider before pouring the rest of the cider over the rabbit. You will need the cider to just cover the meat.

Now for the slow cooking. Turn the heat down so the meat and the sauce just simmers, pop a lid on the saucepan but leave a little gap for the steam to escape.
The slow cooking is going to take three hours, but make sure that you check the pot every half hour or so, turning the meat in the cider.

Prepare a hand full of shallots by removing the skins and have them ready to add to the rabbit. Now when the cooking time is almost completed check the rabbit is cooked by pushing a fork into the meat. If it feels tender it's time to add the shallots and cook for another ten minutes or until the shallots are just tender.

It is at this stage you add a good splash of thick cream to the sauce. This will enrich the sauce and also help to thicken it. With the aid of a spoon taste the creamy sauce. Salt and pepper may be required to bring out the flavours. A little thing that grandmother would do was to pop a pound of pork sausages into the pot half an hour before the rabbit was ready. Sausages cooked in this creamy cider sauce and served with rabbit, happy days!

PORK BRAWN

This is one of my favourite dishes, if made well. Many years ago we would enjoy a freshly made pork brawn that was served up with big chunks of buttered home made bread. Grandmother would always make her own as she always said, "I know what goes into it."

On her trip to the local butcher she would acquire a pigs hock and trotter, and from this she would produce a wonderful bowl of pork brawn. If you ever came to the kitchen door in those days when grandmother was cooking the pork brawn you would be greeted by the aroma of pork, sage, onions and spices that would fill the air. It made you feel hungry just to smell it.

The aroma would be coming from a deep saucepan simmering away on her stove. She would keep a sharp eye on it so not to let the simmering liquid fall below the pork hock, but on the other hand the remaining juices must be reduced so the pork will set. This was a fine art that she had perfected over many years, and there were many comments from grandfather if it was not set firm for his liking.

Grandmother never made the pork cheese in the summer months as her kitchen had only a cold walk in larder. A refrigerator, what was that? The only way to keep things like pork cheeses was to make them in mid-winter. There was little point of making them in the summer months.

I can just see us all now, sitting round the dining room table, with a pork cheese that grandmother had just turned out of the bowl onto a plate. Grandfather giving it a little prod with his knife to see if it was set to his standard. If it was, he gently smiled and cut a slice. Freshly baked bread that had been cooked in the coal-fired oven was placed on the table still warm. With the curtains drawn and the coal fire burning in the grate, grandmother stood up and switched on the radio for it was time for Mrs Dale's diary.

Pork Brawn Often known as Pork Cheese

To make a good home made pork cheese you will need to visit your friendly butcher. What you will need is a pork hock complete with trotter. On your return you will have to find a good size saucepan that will hold the pork and water to cook it in.

Put the pork hock and trotter into the saucepan and just cover it with cold water; next add a chopped medium sized onion, plus a sprig of fresh sage if you have one, also a few black pepper corns will help to add flavour to the finished pork cheese. Once you have added all your bits to the pot its time to put it on the stove and bring to the boil. Once it's up to boiling point turn it down to a simmer.

As the pork slowly cooks, top up with water as required. The pork will take at least three hours on a slow heat to make the hock tender, and when I say tender it will need to fall off the bone.

Once the cooking time is finished gently lift the pork out of the saucepan and place in a dish to cool off. When the pork has cooled down, remove it all from the bone, including the skin. Place it on a chopping board and, with a sharp knife, start chopping disregarding any small bones that you may find. You will, I hope, finish up with almost a puree of pork.

Place this into a large sized bowl, and pour the pork liquid through a fine strainer into the bowl of pork. Add a little seasoning of pepper and salt if needed.

Now the hard bit, you will need a pudding bowl of a good size that will take all the pork and liquid in one go. Once the mixture is cooled down you will be able to place it in the fridge to set. Serve a nice slice of pork cheese with a good splodge of freshly made Colman's mustard.

Rushmore's Restaurant
High Street Heacham
King's Lynn
Norfolk
England

HARES

It was a bit of a thing at Christmas when I was a lad. My grandfather would never eat any of the two roasted cockerels that the family would enjoy for our Christmas lunch. No, for him it was to be a roasted hare.

I can still remember the smell as he skinned it in the kitchen; it was a smell that you could not escape from. In fact it stank the house out. Once the skin was off, it was chopped up into portions and made ready for the oven.

The family on Christmas day was more interested in the two fattened cock birds that were roasted in the oven than grandfather's hare. So he was always left in sole charge of cooking and it goes with out saying that he always managed and you could see the pride on his face as he presented his roasted hare on the table.

All that was many years ago, but hares have paid a big part in my time in the kitchen. As one of four young commis chefs it was our job in the game season to skin and chop them up ready for the oven. The next time that Mr Hare became a big part of my life was the occasion when I went for the job of head chef, at the Black Horse Inn in the village of Castle Rising.

The Inn, at that time, was under going a make over. Not of the plastic type but, very much bringing the old inn back to a real old village pub with a fine restaurant to boot. As I walked into the building, the workmen were still busy bringing it back to a standard of years gone by.

I remember the question that I was asked during the interview that brought a little smile to my face. The new owner was wanting to find a chef that could cook traditional English fayre. "By the way, what would you cook as a garnish for jugged hare?" I could not believe my luck. I thought back to the days as a commis chef and remembered that the head chef always served little forcemeat balls with his jugged hare. To cut the story short, he was impressed and I got the job. Those years at the Black Horse at Castle Rising were some of the happiest years of my life. Very much so as I was head chef there for ten years.

Jugged Hare

Over the ten years at the Black Horse I cooked hundreds of hares and this is my recipe. After years of skinning hares I find it more convenient to order them from the game dealer all ready skinned. Take the hare and lay it on a good chopping board. You will also need a sharp cleaver and a steady hand as hare should be the only meat that is needed in this dish.

Portion the hare into two legs and one nice saddle, leaving the two front legs and the rib cage, which is called the basket, intact. You will find that the rib cage has a skin that protects the lungs and heart do not pierce this as there is a large amount of blood left behind the skin.

I am not a great of lover of following the recipe for jugged hare to the full, as that entails saving the hare's blood to thicken the sauce. With a sharp knife, slit the skin that protects the basket and pour the blood away. Remove the heart and lungs and with a cleaver chop the legs and rib cage into two portions.

Once you have your portions of hare find a good-sized stoneware bowl. Pop the hare into it with four or five bay leaves, ten juniper berries, a few sticks of celery, one onion chopped and a hand full of parsley. Take a cheap bottle of red wine and pour over the hare making sure that all the herbs and hare are well covered. Cover the bowl with cling film and place in the fridge over night so that all the herbs will infuse into the hare.

Next day remove the basin of hare from the fridge, and find yourself a heavy bottomed saucepan. Now for the cooking, take each portion of hare out of the basin pat dry with kitchen paper then place in seasoned flour.

Heat up a frying pan with a little oil and place the hare in the hot oil to seal it. Pour the red wine and herbs into the saucepan and bring up to boiling point. Place the hare into the saucepan and then turn down to a simmer. The hare will require around two or more hours of gentle cooking to make it tender.

Once you are satisfied that the hare is tender its time to thicken the sauce and for this I use, not the blood, but corn flour mixed with water. This is slowly added to obtain the correct consistency. I finish the sauce by checking it for seasoning with salt and pepper, and little double cream stirred well in.

The little forcemeat balls that are served with this dish of jugged hare are simply made by taking sausage meat rolling into small meatballs and dropping them into the sauce 15 minutes before serving. There you have it a traditional dish of Norfolk jugged hare. We still serve it today in my restaurant but I am sad to say not many others do.

PIGEONS

A little time ago we visited a restaurant that offered pigeon breasts as a starter, and having not tasted pigeon for a long time I decided that I would give it a try. After some time had passed we were shown to the table and the starters were presented.

The dish was described, on the menu, as pan-fried pigeon breasts served in a red wine and fresh herb sauce. The two little pigeon breasts were on a small amount of frizzy leaves with a teaspoon full of sauce drizzled around them. I understand that some meats today are served on the pink side, but as I sliced into the breasts one could only say that a good vet could have brought the pigeon back to life.

In the 1970's, when I was chef at the Black Horse at Castle Rising, the local gamekeeper would often bring me twenty pigeons. The kitchen porter at that time had the unpleasant task of preparing the birds. The best way was with a very sharp knife that would be used to remove just the breasts from the pigeons, discarding the rest. The prepared pigeon breasts were put in a thick-bottomed saucepan in which I first always placed a good layer of root vegetables. Carrots, leeks, celery, chopped onions and parsnips, would form the base on which the pigeon breasts would be placed.

Once that had been done, a bottle of cheap red wine would be poured over them and five nice fresh bay leaves added. After a while, the pot would be placed on to the stove and brought to the boil. When this had been achieved it was turned down to a simmer and was left to cook.

After an hour had passed the pot was removed and placed on a trivet to slowly cool down. This cooling down continued to cook the pigeon breasts and when cold you had a breast of pigeon that was as tender as a prime fillet steak. The breasts would then be used to make the pie which was topped with a light shortcrust pastry and served with peas and mashed potatoes that was laced with a rich red wine gravy; a real taste of good country food.

Pigeon Pie

To make the pie its probably best if you obtain the pigeons from a butcher that deals in game. You can cook the bird whole and peal the meat off when its cold as you will get a small amount of meat from the legs.
I understand that for home use you will not be wishing to cook off twenty pigeons, so for a pie say for four persons I would use six birds.

Find a good-sized saucepan and into that cover the bottom with chopped root vegetables, but do not include potatoes. Pop your pigeons in the pan and add a little red wine, top up with water to cover the birds. Next thing to do is to put the saucepan on to the stove and simmer for at least one hour if not a little longer. Pull the pan off the heat and place a plate on top of the pan and leave it to cool down.

When the pigeons have cooled down remove them and start to flake the meat from the carcase. Find yourself a nice pie dish that you think will fit the bill and lay the flaked meat into this.

The next thing that we require to make this dish is a nice rich gravy. Now straining the juices that the pigeons were cooked in into a saucepan can make this. Once this has been done and brought to the boil it can be thickened with a little corn flour. If you wish you can add a spot of red wine and the odd bay leaf at this stage to add a little more flavour.

For the pastry: this wants to be light and when baked to a golden brown will trap the pigeons inside only to be released when you cut into the pie. I once worked with a chef many years ago that would always turn his back on you when he made his pie pastry. His secret has left this world with him years ago but by thinking of the store cupboard that he would have had to use in those days I believe that I have almost perfected his pie pastry. Take 1lb of self-raising flour, add to this a pinch of salt then add 8 ounces of suet and rub well in. The old chef then melted a good knob of butter and this was gently blended in with the other ingredients. Slowly mix to the pastry stage by adding water that has a whole egg beaten into it.

Now that your gravy has had chance to cool down a little pour this over the pigeon meat. I always add the traditional sliced hard boiled eggs at this point but that's up to you. At this stage you roll out the pastry not to thinly please as once cooked we wish for a good thick crust.

With the oven preheated, pop the pie, that you have glazed with brushed egg yolk, into the oven to cook. As soon as the piecrust has turned a golden brown turn the oven down to make sure that the meat is good and hot.

It only remains to phone up a few friends that love the odd helping of pigeon pie served with light fluffy mashed potatoes and a nice glass of red wine.

FRESH WATER FISH

Those people that know me, understand the passion I have for fishing. It not only gives me the excitement of battling with nature but also total relaxation. Once many years ago I caught a nice sized carp and regret to this day bringing it home to cook. Nowadays I always return fresh water fish back into the river and would never dream of cooking them, but a friend of mine who lives in a cottage just a few yards from a mill stream told me that he had a corking good recipe for fresh water fish and would let me have all the details on our next fishing trip.

The day came and as we settled down by the river I asked him to reveal his secret recipe. "Well, say you catch a good sized tench," he said. " What you do is this. Take the fish and remove its head and tail, then gut it. Give it a good wash in salted water and lay it on some kitchen paper to dry off. The next thing is very important. Get yourself two wooden boards made of a soft wood like pine; lay the fish on one of the boards. You will need to add to the fish the juice of one lemon a little salt and two turns on the pepper mill, also a pinch of fresh dill would be great. After you have done all this you pop the other wooden board on top of the seasoned fish. OK so far?"

By a nodding of my head I must have indicated that I was still with him. "Now comes the best bit. Gently wrap the two wooden boards that contain the fish in tin foil but make sure that there are no little holes left in the parcel to allow any of the juices to escape. Then all you have to do is place it in a medium hot oven, say for not less than one hour." "Well that sounds good. So what happens next?" I asked.

"Once you are happy that the fish is well cooked, take your time to remove it from the oven, slowly unwrap the tin foil from the boards holding it." By this time my mind was working overtime. What was the fish going to taste like? Was this a way of injecting flavour into fresh water fish that normally tastes of the river bottom and very little else?

In my mind I could see the fish laying trapped between the two wooden boards, steam coming from the perfectly cooked river tench, a sweet fragrance was in the air of dill and lemon juice. "Go on tell me," I begged "I bet the fish tastes good."

Then he turned and said "No. No. Don't be stupid! You don't eat the fish. Bin that and eat the boards." It goes with out saying that as far as I am concerned you leave fresh water fish in the river, unless you catch a nice plump stream rainbow trout and that's another matter.

Trout with Brancaster Mussels

Take your fresh rainbow trout and I normally allow one nice fish per person. Gut your fish, remove the head, wash in cold running water and dry the fish with kitchen paper.

The next thing is to pop the trout into a little seasoned flour before placing it in a frying pan that has been gently heated with a knob of butter in it. Dust off any excess flour and place the trout into the hot butter. It's always best if you can keep the fish moving for a few minutes to prevent it sticking to the pan.

Once you feel that the trout has cooked on that side gently turn it over and cook the other side for the same time. Remove it from the pan and lay it on a plate and place in a low heated oven to keep warm.

Take the pan in which you have just cooked your fish, pour off any butter that is left and wipe dry with paper. Replace it on the stove with a small amount of fresh butter, add to this a little very finely chopped onion and turn up the heat but only to soften the onion do not allow the onion to brown.

Add to the pan say ten nice mussels that have been scraped and bearded. Turn the heat up and pour into the pan a glass of dry white wine, swill the pan around and cover it with a lid. The mussels will only take a few minutes to cook and you can tell they are done when their shells are fully open.

Please do not use any that remain closed as these are unfit to eat. Pull the pan off the heat and thicken the sauce. You can do this by adding a mixture of flour and butter that has been blended together to make a paste. Add a little at a time and use a small whisk to make a lump free sauce, which will thicken slightly to a thin cream like consistency.

Remove your warm trout from the oven and place onto a plate, now you add the cooked open mussels placing them around the fish. Finish off by pouring the creamy white sauce onto the fish. Two flavours: one of the river trout and the other from the sea. What more could you ask for?

A BRACE OF ROASTED PHEASANTS

 It was a very cold day in December. I had planned to go beating at Sandringham. When I arrived there had been a hard frost overnight and the ground was covered in a crisp white sheen. You certainly don't go beating for the payment that you receive at the end of the day. What you do go for is a day away from ringing phones, and the friendship that seems to take place whenever you gather men together.

It was not long before we were all in the game trailer. There must have been ten to fifteen beaters including a few of the under gamekeepers and four or five gundogs. There is only one thing you have to remember and that is to sit well away, if possible, from the dogs because when the dogs get wet, they emit a pungent smell as only dogs do. However that's part and parcel of a days beating.

It was not long before we had arrived at the area that had been selected for the first shoot of the day. As the trailer slowly makes its way down the field, it will stop and drop off a couple of men every few yards or so. As we all line up I normally survey the terrain ahead of me. On this occasion it was a field of sugar beet and that I don't mind. It's a lot better that working your way through brambles and pine trees which are often impenetrable to man or beast.

The nod is given and we are moving off. "Keep it straight, chaps." is the only indication of the line having a bow in it and then you will hear the voice of one of the many under game keepers that form part of the line. Sticks are being thrashed on the beet tops and it is now your chance to emit the strangest of vocal sounds that is humanly possible. Multiply this by the number of men in the line and for the game it has the intended effect, sending them up in the direction of the waiting guns. As the line of stick thrashing, howling men moves slowly forward the grounded birds take to the wing. On this drive a couple of guns were walking twenty or more yards behind us. They are there to bag any birds that decide to take flight and fly back over the line. As the drive proceeds we hear the sound of the guns going into action. We have probably thrashed our way across almost a mile and are now in sight of the guns and the first drive of the morning for us is over.

If we have done our job properly, then the birds will have gone over the guns, but now its back to the trailer and on to the next shoot of the day. Normally around one o'clock we stop for lunch. The house sends a van that contains a large container of soup, and on a cold day the soup is appreciated. A selection of drinks are offered also, and then its time to find yourself a cosy corner and discover what delights, if any, the wife has packed you up.

The days shooting finishes well before the light starts to fade, and its then back to the yard where it all started. Just time to say your goodbyes and drive back home to check the answer phone for all the phone calls that you have missed while you have been out shouting at the top of your voice and banging a stick.

Roasted Pheasants
Served with Sticky Red Cabbage
and Red Wine Gravy

The great debate regarding hanging of pheasant, I believe, is a choice that you have to make yourself. My preference is to allow the birds to hang, weather permitting, for about a week or slightly longer. This must be done in a cool well-ventilated area. I feel that the flavour is greatly enhanced by doing this. I must say that I am glad that the days of hanging game until it almost turns bad has, I hope, long gone.

A tip when buying pheasants is always, even if oven ready, make sure they still have the legs on. This is so you can look at the spurs on the bird. Short spurs indicate that the birds are young and not left over from last years shooting season.

To prepare the birds, that is one cock and one hen, for the oven I normally remove any of the fine feathers and stubble that has been left by the plucker. I also make sure that the birds are washed in cold water and are dried well with a clean cloth. I like to tie the legs of the birds together with string. It helps to keep them in shape during the roasting.

The next thing is to find a roasting tray, place the pheasants, breast side up, in the tray and coat with oil or my favourite pork dripping. You can if you wish put a couple of streaky bacon rashers on top of each breast and pop half an onion in each bird. The oven should be at a medium setting and when the required temperature is obtained, place the tray of pheasant into the oven.

The birds will require around thirty to forty minutes cooking. After, say twenty minutes, I like to turn the birds over. This can be done with the aid of a good strong carving fork, and then turn the oven down slightly. When you feel that the pheasant is almost cooked you can test with the aid of a thin knife. Push the blade well into the thigh, if anything other than pure juices runs out then you need to cook the birds a little longer. After you are happy that the pheasants are cooked to your liking remove from the roasting tray and set aside to rest in a warm place.

Now for the red wine gravy; gently remove as much fat as you can and save this as it makes a wonderful dripping for sauté potatoes. Next put a spoonful of flour in the roasting tray and with the aid of a wooden spoon mix it in with the pheasant juices to make a paste. When this is done place over a low heat and stir in about half a pint of chicken stock.

The aim is to blend the paste and stock together to form the gravy, if the gravy is getting a little too thick add a spot more chicken stock and then pour in a splash of red wine. Let the gravy simmer for a few minutes, using the wooden spoon to incorporate any encrusted meat juices that may be stuck on the bottom of the tray.

The thickness of the pan made gravy is a matter of choice. Once you feel that the correct consistency has been obtained pass through a fine strainer into a saucepan. Lastly add a small knob of butter and correct the seasoning if required. To present the dish take four large white plates, with the aid of a good sharp knife remove the legs of the pheasants and place one on each plate. Then slice through the breasts to give you four portions, and place a breast next to the leg. Place a portion of sticky red cabbage, recipe below, at the side of the presented birds and pour a little of the gravy around the pheasant. I always serve the cock birds to the gentlemen and the hen birds to the ladies whenever possible. Lastly, at the table, offer a sauceboat of the red wine gravy and a sauceboat of freshly made bread sauce.

Sticky Red Cabbage

Sticky red cabbage is one of those dishes that goes well with game, but in the restaurant we also serve it with pork fillet.

Take yourself a medium sized red cabbage and slice it very finely. Next find a saucepan that will take the cabbage, add a diced small onion, also add 8ozs of brown sugar, a pinch of salt and a litre of orange juice and mix well and that's it. Dead easy.

The cooking time once the cabbage has been brought to the boil is long and slow. It will require a good hour if not longer. Red cabbage seems to take a long time to cook, so you will need to keep an eye on it. Once the cabbage is cooked very little juice should be left in the pan. You should finish up with bootifull sticky red cabbage ready to be served with your roasted game birds or it can be eaten cold with cold meats.

Pan made Gravy

Gone are the days when I was sent down the road on a Sunday to ask Mrs Jones if mother could borrow your meat to make our gravy. I always say that many a good dish has been a great disaster because of the failure to make a real pan made gravy. The small amount of effort needed is very little to ask after you have gone to all the trouble of cooking the meat to perfection.

What you need to do to make gravy from the meat juices is to gently pour off any fat that may be in the pan. Place the pan on a low heat on the stove and with a whisk give the pan a good stir to dislodge any of the little bits stuck to the sides. Once this has been done add a little plain flour and whisk well in to form a roux.

Slowly add a small amount of water or light chicken stock if you are making game gravy. As you add the water keep stirring with the whisk incorporating all the flakes of pan juices. You will need to add just the right amount of water or stock to obtain the thickness of gravy that you want. Once this has been achieved add seasoning as required. The art of good gravy is to finish up with a liquid of rich colour that will do justice to perfectly cooked meat.

MUSSELS

In the restaurant we all look forward to the start of the mussel season. It starts in early September but even with the thoughts of serving up bowls of freshly cooked mussels in their shells coated in a creamy white wine sauce has to be left until the weather has turned a little cooler. It's the same warm weather that brings the season to an abrupt end in April. That depicts the mussel season for me.

The mussels that we use come from Brancaster. That's just around the coast from the restaurant, so we can buy fresh daily, and it's the commis chef's nightmare when he arrives on duty to find a nice big bag of barnacled covered mussels waiting for him.

Not too bad for a few weeks but it wears a bit thin after the first month. Oh, I feel so sorry for him as he leans over the sink scraping away with my old oyster knife and by the time that the season has almost finished he has just about perfected the art of mussel cleaning.

We use the mussels as a starter served in a sauce of white wine and lemon juice and I must say that they are one of our best sellers. Cooked to order, it becomes a bit of a pain especially on a Saturday night when the restaurant is heaving and full to the rafters. Never mind they say you have to suffer pain to get the gain??

In the season we must cook tonnes of mussels and use gallons of white wine, parsley, sliced shallots, and the juices from hundreds of lemons. You will find lots of good restaurants in Norfolk serving fresh local mussels on their menus. This I believe shows that people are looking for fresh food that is in season, gathered by hand, cooked, and fresh from the sea.

Mussels in White Wine

You don't have to be master chef to cook and serve mussels in white wine; even a commis chef with a love for the job can perfect it. One thing you must acquire from the supplier of your mussels is a little scrap of paper. This is a legal requirement. To put it in a nutshell, it must by law state his name and the date he sold you the mussels. These little forms have to be kept for three months.

I am pleased to say that I remember the days when you just walked on to the mussel beds at low tide filled your sack, went home and cooked them for your tea. Sadly forty years on, this has long gone.

This is my commis chef's recipe for mussels in white wine. After scraping the barnacles off and removing what we call the beards, that's that little bit of hair that the mussel hangs on to the rocks with. To remove get hold of it, give it a good pull and it will come away from the shell.

Now that we have the mussels clean, find yourself a nice saucepan of medium size, and pop it onto a good heat. Add a knob of butter and then when the butter has melted add about three small shallots or a small onion very finely diced. Turn up the heat and once the onion has just started to colour add your mussels.

Keep the heat on full blast and add around one cup of dry white wine. Make sure that you give the mussels a good stir, next add a squeeze of fresh lemon juice and a sprinkling of fresh chopped parsley. With the heat on high pop the lid on the saucepan and give it a good shake.

The mussels only require a few minutes cooking. Just make sure that all the shells are open and disregard those that remain closed, as they may not be good. This dish will not require salt but only a sprinkling of black pepper. Just one little tip if the sauce is very thin, then add a spot of corn flour that has been mixed with a little water. This will help to thicken the sauce.

To present this dish use a large white bowl. When the mussels are cooked and ready pop them into the bowl and pour the sauce over them. Add a good wedge of lemon on the side of the bowl and then put a pinch of chopped parsley over the mussels. Now that's the commis chef's mussels in white wine.

A SAUCE FOR FISH

It's very pleasing to be offered a nice portion of freshly baked cod with a little sauce that tastes slightly of the dish that it is supposed to accompany. The intended sauce must not be so strong that it could over power the fish that you are using.

Often I will make a quick sauce just to add a little interest to what could be a bland fish dish. This can be as simple as opening a small tin of chopped tomatoes, and adding these plus a little chopped fresh basil to the fish in the final stages of cooking. This is a very easy way of spicing up a fish or salmon fillet as tomato and basil goes very well with both.

When you buy your fish ask the fishmonger for a small amount of fish bones from filleted soles but make sure that they are fresh. Find a good-sized saucepan and place the fish bones together with half a chopped onion into it. Fill the saucepan half full and make sure that the bones are below the water.

Place the pan on the stove; bring to the boil and then turn down to a simmer. The fish bones will probably send up a whitish froth that is best removed with a ladle. The stock will only require around thirty minutes. Any longer and you will finish up with a pot of glue.

Take another saucepan and add a few ounces of soft margarine and pop on to a low heat to melt. Once this has been achieved add the same weight in flour and mix well together with a whisk. Now it's time to add the fish stock and this is best done after you have strained it through a fine hair strainer. Slowly add the stock a little at a time, use the whisk to mix it together to make a smooth white fish sauce.

It's a combination of the correct amount of heat and fish stock going into the pan at one time, that will give you a perfect white sauce. As the sauce cooks out you will find it may take more stock. You will, I hope, finish up with a sauce that will coat the back of a ladle. Last of all is to correctly season the sauce with salt and white pepper, and if you wish you can add a pinch or two of chopped parsley.

EELS

Fishing for eels was one of the favourite things that we did if Roger and I decided we would like to stay out all night. Eel fishing is best done at night for some reason. Mother would pack us up lots of sandwiches and cold drinks that would, if we were careful, last us through to the morning. Of course they never did as most of the sandwiches were eaten within a few hours of arriving at the river.

 You often caught the odd eel when trying to catch other fish, but on these occasions we were only after eels, and that's the reason that we were fishing at night. Slimy old things are eels but, for the dedicated few that like them, they are delicious. So with that in mind we were armed with two good stiff rods and strong line that, if required, would pull in Moby Dick if we were lucky enough to catch him.

We decided to set up on our favourite spot, but first we would introduce our secret weapon. That was two tins of cat food that Roger said his mother would not miss because the cat had died a few weeks ago.

The thing to do with the tins was to punch holes into them thus releasing the smell of the cat food into the water. These were placed in the areas where we thought eels would be. Next we baited up with two or three good size garden worms on special eel hooks and cast our bait in the area where we had introduced the tins of cat food. It was often not long before we were pulling in eels of all sizes, but once they were on the bank then that's when your problems began.

Have you ever tried to unhook an eel in the dark? It was often a bit of a job, but after a few night fishing trips we soon both became experts in the art of unhooking them. Many a time, Roger and I arrived home before mother and father had gone to bed. Maybe the riverbank was not the place for two young lads, especially as the river was not that far from the church graveyard. It was often the ringing of the bells at midnight that made our minds up for us and as long as we had a few good size eels in the old cloth bag we were happy.

Eels with Mash and Parsley Sauce

There are many ways of cooking eels but the way we seemed to prefer was cooking the eels in a saucepan with a little onion and serving on a bed of creamy mashed potatoes and laced with a tasty parsley sauce.

Father would clean the eel and, after removing the head, chop the eel into two inch pieces. You can, if you are used to doing it, skin the eel before cooking it but if not, it's a not too fiddly job once cooked.

In a good-sized saucepan slice one onion and, if you have one, one small bay leaf. Add these to the pan with the chopped up eel, and add just sufficient milk to cook the eels. Place the saucepan on the stove and bring to the simmer.

Cooking time depends on the size of the eel portions, so after twenty minutes test with a sharp knife. With experience you will soon know when to remove from the heat.

The potatoes that will make the mash must be put on the stove around the same time as you start cooking the eel. I will come back to the potatoes in a little while.

Meanwhile find another saucepan so you can make the parsley sauce. Pop the saucepan on a low heat and add a good knob of butter. Once this has melted add a little flour and combine the flour with the butter to form the base of the parsley sauce. Next add the infused milk, a little at a time, to the saucepan. It's often best to use a wire whisk to make a smooth white sauce, add the milk until the sauce is smooth and at the correct thickness.

Once you have done this it's time to add a good handful of chopped parsley to the sauce and all that's left to do is season the sauce to your taste with a little salt and ground white pepper.

Now it's time to perfect the mashed potatoes. Once you have grated the potatoes add a small amount of warm milk and if possible a little freshly grated nutmeg, this will give a lift to the simple spud. Just a word of warning add the milk in small amounts, so you finish up with a mash that is still firm.

To plate up the dish pop your mashed potatoes in the middle of a nice plate, place a portion of cooked eel around the mash, then pour over the rich parsley sauce over the eels, and tuck in.

COCKLES

When I think of cockles it reminds of my happy days as a child, the memory of walking miles out towards the sea at Heacham in Norfolk. Sunday was the day that we would rise early with the hopes that a trip to Heacham was imminent.

This was to be decided by the weather. Father would walk to the front and then to the back of the house with his head firmly pointing skywards. As children, we knew that any sign of a cloud in the sky, whatever its colour, would put thoughts in father's mind that there might be a chance of rain.

When he had decided that all was clear, a nod was given to mother to start making the sandwiches that we always stopped to eat, in those days, on the green that bordered the road outside the gates at Sandringham.

Once lunch had been consumed, we all piled into the old Humber car that father owned at the time and then it was off to Heacham south beach. The basic tools required for obtaining a good feed of cockles were very simple. A sack to carry them in and a supply of old rakes on short handles that would be used to find the cockles that lay just below the surface of the sand.

Father said that he always knew were the best cockles were to be found. It always seemed to my sister and me that this involved walking miles. Once we had found what father had decided to be the spot, then it was all hands to the pumps, rakes, spades and often just bare hands were used to uncover the fruits of the sea.

If that spot did not reveal as much as we expected then father always had another place in mind, just half a mile from this one. By late afternoon the sack was full, or held at least enough for a good feed. The tide was coming in at a rate of knots and it was time to make a hasty retreat back to the shore and head for home.

Cockles With Vinegar

On returning from our cockling trip, mother would find the old pail that was used for soaking the cockles. After giving them a good wash under the tap, she would put them into the bucket, top it up with fresh cold water, and then mother would add a small amount of flour. This I was told helped to remove any sand from them over night.

The bucket would be placed in a cool place until the next day when the water was drained off. Then a quick wash under the tap and hey presto the cockles were now ready for the cooking pot.

Father had obtained a large saucepan on his travels and this was ideal for cooking cockles. It was filled halfway with water and allowed to boil. Once boiling point was reached the cockles were dropped in and the lid was placed on. After a few moments father would lift the lid, and then pop it back on again. "Just a tad longer," was father's comment.

It was explained to us children that you have to wait until the shells are just opened, and then it's into the strainer. While the cockles were still in their shells they would be placed in bowls ready for a good sprinkling of vinegar. Perfection was to be found in this simple dish from the sea.

As we all sat down to tea the cockles were consumed with lashings of buttered brown bread. Memories of having walked miles were soon forgotten, and thoughts crept in of what next Sunday's weather would bring.

CRABS

I suppose that wherever crabs are caught, people will say that theirs are the best. But as we all know the sweetest fleshed crabs are caught, off Cromer, in Norfolk. It was a warm summer's day many years ago that grandfather decided to go crabbing and I was asked if I would like to go with him. This was an opportunity not to be missed, a day out at the seaside.

We had to go by bus, as grandfather never owned a car. He did have an old trade bike that had a wooden box fitted on the front. This in its time was the carrier of many things; corn for the chickens, coke from the local gas works, that was used to heat the copper in the back yard. From this copper came the hot water that filled the tin bath that came out every Friday night.

All these goods and many more were balanced in that old box on the trade bike. It was, I am afraid to say, suggested that I could sit in the box with my legs dangling outside. However, because of the distance grandfather would have had to pedal, he ruled out that idea.

Grandfather, on this occasion, was dressed up for our trip to the seaside. He was wearing his black suit with a stiff collar that was held in place with a little brass stud and of course his highly prized and polished black leather boots. In his hand he carried an old canvas bag, plus a long stick with a metal hook on the end. When the bus arrived, we climbed aboard and made ourselves comfortable for the journey of almost twenty or so miles to the coast.

On arrival at the seaside, grandfather insisted that we set about our task as quickly as possible as the tide was on the turn. I followed him as we removed our boots and socks and rolled up our trousers to stop them getting wet. Grandfather had put me in charge of carrying the boots that had had our socks neatly placed inside them. So we headed out to where there was a large pool of shallow water that contained a clump of rocks.

"Hold the bag, boy, while I have a go." This is where the long stick with the metal hook came into play. Grandfather was no newcomer to the art of crabbing and it was not long after, with a little poking and prodding with his stick, that the first of many fine crabs found their way into his old canvas bag.

I don't know if it was all the excitement of seeing so many crabs, but I did what grandfather said was unforgivable and I would probably never be allowed to come on another crabbing trip. I could only look in horror as grandfather's boots slipped out of my hands and became submerged in a foot of salty water.

He didn't say a lot as we walked slowly back to catch the bus home. Until this day, I can remember the squelching sounds that those black boots made.

Cromer Crab Salad

When grandfather arrived home he would have had to cook the crabs and then set about the task of removing the dead mans fingers and the long job of dressing the crabs. Nowadays I find it's better to buy the crabs in the shell already cooked and dressed.

To present a nice Cromer crab starter in the restaurant we use a metal ring into which you place the dressed crab. To present this dish for the table it is best done on a good size white plate. Around the plate, arrange a selection of fresh salad leaves. You can buy a small bag of these from any supermarket.

Once this has been done, place the metal ring in the centre of the plate and gently fill with the fresh crab. When you have filled the ring, add a little lemon mayonnaise to the crab. If you want to go the whole hog, grate a cucumber and gently add a swirl of this on top of the mayonnaise. Finish off the presentation with a little diced tomato that has been added to a drop of good quality olive oil and pour this over the salad leaves. It now just requires a wedge of lemon and the removal of the metal ring. There you have it, a dish of the sweetest of crabs from the rock pools of Cromer.

FLAT FISH
Dabs and Plaice

On warm summer mornings in the school holidays, my friend Roger and I would often go what we called dabbing. We didn't use a rod and line, but a contraption of our own invention that we had perfected and as youngsters we saw no harm in it.

The contraption that we had designed and crafted was a bamboo pole, almost ten feet long, with a six-inch nail firmly stuck in to one end. The nail had to be heated and made into an arrow shape and this was done while father was at work.

With father's blow lamp on full blast you could heat up the nail until it became so hot you could then, with a large hammer, hit the nail to produce the arrow shape. Once this had been achieved and once the nail had cooled down you then set to work with father's hacksaw. By sawing in the correct way barbs were made. It only remained to fix it into the long bamboo pole, and there it was, just the job for a day's dab fishing.

Unfortunately the production of dab poles came to a abrupt end as one day Roger left father's blow lamp pointing in the wrong direction, and there was no way that father would miss seeing that half the wooden shed was missing.

With a pole each we would set off together along the riverbank that ran behind the sea wall. The river led into the sea at some stage and all sorts of fish found their way into the river from the sea. Many a time we borrowed mother's sunglasses and these were very good especially on a very sunny day. Without them you had to place your hand over your forehead to deflect the sunlight shining on the water.

The flat fish could be found lying on the riverbed and were often half hidden with silt. But you soon became an expert in spotting them. Once you had then you went into action with the pole. Slowly you would lower the pole over the fish and taking aim you would thrust the pole into the fish. More often than not, just as the pole was released, a cloud of silt would be the only thing left, as the fish scooted away to the other side of the river well out of reach of two young lads.

On a good day we would get five or six dabs and if we were lucky we would bag a few plaice as well. Also there were the times when we would spot a big old dab just a little too far out for us to get a good clear shot at. Of course we never gave up without trying and so we came up with the idea that if Roger would hold my arm and I would lean out as far as possible and with a little calculation I should be able to get the fish.

It was agreed and as Roger held my arm I carefully leant out until I was almost within striking range. Slowly the pole came up and I was locked on to the target.

Then it happened, I myself put it down, now that I have had many years to think about it, to the fact that I was almost twice as heavy as Roger. It seemed to happen in a split second. There was an almighty splash as we both fell forwards into the river.

On that day we both got more than we had bargained for. It was at least two miles back to our homes and as we walked home there was silence and the next fishing trip was the last thing on our minds.

Dabs Cooked in Butter

To prepare the fish for the pan you need to remove the head of the flatfish. Once that has been done you can, if you wish, remove the brown skin. This is achieved by nicking the skin near the tail; this will give you just sufficient grip to pull the skin away. Slowly pull upwards and the skin will peel off.

When cooking any flat fish dabs, plaice, soles, I am a great believer in keeping it simple. A fresh sole just cooked in butter with a squeeze of lemon juice is all you need. No sauce will ever replace the delicate flavour of the fresh fish.

So with that in mind, find yourself a large frying pan and place it on the stove. Add a good knob of butter to the pan; making sure that the butter is not burning, by adjusting the heat. With your flatfish prepared, dust it well with flour and place in the pan. With the help of a large spatula turn the fish over, so the other side will cook.

When you feel that the fish is cooked, and this can be tested with the aid of a sharp knife, then add a good squeeze of lemon juice and if you wish a little chopped parsley to add that extra flavour.

To serve: gently lift the fish onto a plate, and pour a little of the butter and juices over the fish. Add a round or two of brown bread and butter to make it into a meal fit for a king.

THE LARDER

In the 1950's most houses had a small larder under the stairs or, as in our house, a walk in larder. Normally these were painted white to help keep them cool. Also there was, if you were lucky, a slab of marble that helped keep things like cheese cool.

As you opened the door to the larder the items within would amaze you. Often a shelf or two would be fixed to hold jars of bottled jams, the odd jar of samphire that was bottled in July, and maybe peaches that we hoped would last to Christmas.

But it was down on the marble shelf you would find the most interesting goods. Cheeses covered with a contraption that was made of muslin cloth, the leftovers from the Sunday roast covered with a cloth that protected it from the flies.

However most foods were kept in tins. Old Smith's Crisps tins were a favourite of mothers and these were perfect for the storage of the baking days treats. Food in those days, before the refrigerator, was kept in the walk in pantry and had to be fresh and was normally eaten on the day of purchase. There was no once a week visit to the supermarket to top up the freezer or fridge in those days.

People like my mother had to plan the menu and shopped daily. The days in this country of shopping on a daily basis have well gone, so has the walk in larder. We are lucky that in the house where we live there still is one.

No longer are the shelves filled with jars of peaches, or jars of samphire waiting to be opened on a cold winter's night. They would be drained off and placed between freshly baked bread hopefully bringing back memories of the summer.

Gone also are the Smith's Crisps tin that would have contained the remains of mother's Christmas cake. In the place of all this stands a white refrigerator, soulless and as cool as a cucumber. I am certain nobody will ever write about memories of the fridge aren't you?

Rushmore's Restaurant High Street Heacham

APPLES AND BLACKBERRIES

Whenever the autumn comes around and winter is just starting to rear its head my thoughts always turn to remembering dear old Ingoldisthorpe Manor hotel.

The manor house sat on the top of the hill and was turned into a hotel of the four-star standard many years before I arrived to work in its kitchens. I worked firstly as second chef then for a year or so as head chef. The manor was set in large well cared for gardens and at the rear was the most wonderful walled vegetable garden, which provided us with most of the daily requirements of the kitchen.

It was during my time at the manor that I met a lady by the name of Elsie Kirk. It was Elsie's job to arrive in the morning and cook breakfasts for the guests that were staying in the hotel. We were given many awards in those days from the AA and also the RAC and often you would read that a London newspaper had given the hotel a write up in one of its food columns. It was that sort of place.

Mrs Kirk's breakfasts were a treat not to miss but also not to be missed was her apple and blackberry pie. Every Sunday Elsie would, after finishing cooking breakfasts, start the preparation for a dish that would probably sell out before we had finished lunch service, namely the famous pie.

People would travel many a mile each Sunday for the pie. As they arrived for lunch they would ask the headwaiter to save them a portion of apple and blackberry pie and woe betide the waiting staff when the pie was sold out.

The pie was offered with thick Bird's custard and served in a nice white bowl. The chunky slices of apple and blackberries were trapped below a light golden pastry. Served warm, the scent of this combination arrived at your table well before the pie did...

The manor held many good and happy memories for me, but the best and lasting one will always be Mrs Kirk's apple and blackberry pie.

Mrs Kirk's Apple and Blackberry Pie

 After breakfast Elsie would start to prepare the apples ready for the pie. She would normally use Bramleys as these were now in season. Once a bowl of peeled apples was done Elsie would find a large saucepan, place it on the stove and fill it with not only the apples but also a basket of freshly picked blackberries.

Slowly the apples and blackberries are cooked together to infuse. The timing is important, as the apples must remain firm. Elsie would know the exact time to remove the saucepan from the heat. I suppose this came from years of cooking blackberry and apple pie.

While the apples were cooking she would have made the pastry and placed it in the fridge to rest. Once the pastry had had its resting time it was placed on to a cold marble slab and rolled out to the correct size. It had to fit over the large tray that would contain the hot apples and blackberries.

Once the fruit had been cooked to perfection, it was strained of any excess juices and placed into the baking tray. It was then left in a cool place to cool down before adding the pastry crust. After around an hour Elsie would gently roll out the pastry and pop it over the tray to trap the apples and blackberries inside, a good brushing with egg yolk and it was ready to go into the oven.

After the delegated cooking time, that only Elsie knew, the pie would be removed and the kitchen would be transformed into a winter wonder land with the scent of sweet apples and blackberries permeating the air.

The only sauce that she would serve with her pie would be Bird's custard made with milk and a good splash of fresh double cream that she would add at the last minute.

I have returned to the grounds where the manor once stood. In the 1980's it was burnt to the ground and destroyed. The famous hotel stands no more. Now on its site is an estate of houses.

It was late October when I last visited the site and the mist was just coming down over the houses. The well cared for gardens had gone, as also had the large willow tree under which people had afternoon tea in the summer time. In my mind's eye I was trying to work out were the manor had stood, a very sad time.

Then something came drifting from the area where I imagined the hotel had stood. It was a sweet scent of apples and blackberries. Mrs Kirk's apple and blackberry pie I presume?

NORFOLK DUMPLINGS

No book on Norfolk foods would ever be complete without a recipe for the county's traditional dish of Norfolk dumplings. Many years ago these were called swimmers or floaters. Unlike the dumpling that is made with suet, the Norfolk dumpling is made with a bread dough and while cooking gently floats in the pot.

Often bakers would sell the Norfolk dumpling and I can remember being sent off to the bakers as a young lad to collect them in time for grandmother to pop them into the beef stew to be served up at dinner-time.

Dinner time as many called it in those days was in fact lunch, normally served around midday, and it was the time that most people sat down together and had the main meal of the day.

Being sent to get the dumplings from the bakers in mid-winter was a thing that was not always on my list of best things to do on a freezing cold day. But once grandmother had found me there was no escaping. She would make me put on my long coat. This was followed by a hand knitted scarf, and then to make sure that my little ears didn't get the winter chill another large scarf would be wrapped around my head and face making look as if I had just arrived from the south pole. On my return with the dumplings I was always given sixpence for going.

Come the day when grandfather told me that we were having lamb stew and Norfolk dumplings for dinner. This information was music to my ears. It was a day when the weather outside was as bad as it gets. You always could tell if it was really cold as the frost was on the inside of the windows in the kitchen.

Even the dog never moved away from the fire on that sort of day.

Time had come for me to be sent to the bakers. But for grandmother, I was nowhere to be seen. Not even sixpence was going to get me out of my hiding place in the chicken shed that day.

After an hour or so with only a handful of chickens for company I decided to leave my hiding place only to be met by grandfather. He had been sent to find me. "Come on, boy. Dinner's on the table and its getting cold." Arriving in the house he must have picked up on the smell of the chickens. "Go and wash your self, boy, before you sit down you don't smell too sweet.

To my great surprise there on the plate was not only a rich plateful of lamb stew but sitting on top of it was a big steaming Norfolk dumpling,

Grandfather explained that as I was nowhere to be found grandmother had made her own and saved herself sixpence to boot as well.

Grandmother's Norfolk Dumplings

For a family of four.
2lb of plain flour
pinch of salt
one pint of milk
a pinch of sugar
about 1oz of dried yeast
2oz of butter

Grandmother would put the flour and salt into a good size mixing bowl. She would then gently heat the milk and butter until the butter was melted. Then she added the sugar to the milk and butter and allowed the mix to cool till it was only lukewarm. She would then sprinkle on the dried yeast and set aside for ten to fifteen minutes to go frothy. Next the job of pouring the mixture into the flour and with her hands she would mix it into a firm dough.

After this she would turn the dough out onto a floured table and knead the dough till it became smooth. It was then put back into a clean bowl and covered with a damp cloth. Now it was placed aside in a warm place to rise and double its size.

Then grandmother would remove the dough and knead it again. Once that had been done it was shaped into balls the size of small chicken eggs, and once again left to rise. After all this palaver grandmother would have the dumplings ready to drop into the pot simmering lamb stew. Cooking time was around fifteen minutes.

So in a way I was sorry that I never again received sixpence for going to the bakers. But I always said that grandmother's Norfolk dumplings were better than the bakers, especially in the wintertime.

BAKING DAY

Before the days of mass buying from the local supermarket most ladies of the house set aside one day for baking. This would be the day that most of the fancy cakes and special treats for the family would be cooked.

If you had the privilege of being allowed in grandmother's kitchen on her baking day you would have seen her with her flowered smock on and busy at her baking tasks. Old tins that held her plain and self-raising flours were clearly marked. On the scrubbed kitchen table, a large rolling pin lay ready, a knife that grandfather had made sure was sharp by giving it a good going over on the back door stone-step the night before.

On her baking list were apple pies and any fruit pies that were in season at the time. The apple pies were of course made with cooking apples that we as children had picked from the old tree at the end of the garden. Also she would make rock cakes, that I can assure you lived up to their name; a rich Norfolk treacle tart that lasted no longer than the day it was baked on; and grandmother's special baking day treat vinegar cake.

Vinegar cake was one of those recipes that had been handed down from mother to daughter and my grandmother had perfected it. This was amazing remembering that the only oven that she had was coal fired.

In the 1950's grandfather had a drinking pal named Fred that worked on the docks. This was in the days when all the hold of the ship had to be unloaded by hand and often you would see a bag of dark brown sugar, and items that were in short supply at the time left on the kitchen table. From this sugar grandmother would make a dark treacle toffee, that once set was broken into small lumps and left on the kitchen table for all to help themselves. Woe betide any person, including old Mrs Dingle, from next door that had false teeth. Grandmother always remarked as Mrs Dingle popped a large bit into her mouth, "That will shut her up for a few hours."

When she was cooking the toffee it always smelt like the vinegar cake cooking as both contained vinegar and it's sharp smell filled the kitchen.

Vinegar Cake

Grandmother would have a large mixing bowl, you know the type, made out of concrete and requiring all of two persons to lift it. Into the bowl she would put one lb (450g) of self-raising flour and 8 oz (225g) of butter that may have come from Fred that worked on the docks. With her fingers she would work this into a crumb like mixture. Once this had being achieved grandmother would add to the bowl 8 oz (225g) of raisins, 8 oz (225g) of sultanas and also 8 oz (225g) of caster sugar, and these would be well mixed in.

Next add 8 fluid ounces (180ml) of milk to a large jug with 2tbsp of vinegar. In a cup mix together 1tsp of bicarbonate of soda with 1tbsp of milk and then add it to the milk and vinegar and stir it in.

Stir this mixture into the flour and fruit working in all the flour. Pour the cake mixture into a well-buttered cake tin and pop into the oven for 30 minutes and then turn the heat down and slowly bake for another hour on a low heat. You can place a bit of greased paper on top to stop it becoming too dark on the top. Remove from the tin and cool on a wire rack. Once the cake is cold store in an old Smiths Crisp tin if you have one.

FOOTBALL

Football is one of those games that has been of little interest to me over the years, but I well remember the words "I think its all over, well it is now." I am referring to the World Cup football. As England's hopes always seemed to go pear shaped the commis chef promised me that soon the kitchen would return to normality, and the continuing talk of Beckham and England's progress would stop, and in its place would be kitchen talk. Questions like: "Why has my hollandaise split?" It's the sort of language that I understand rather than the finer points of Beckham's hair-style.

The commis chef, and the young lad that washes up for us are more or less of the same age. It came to light that, when the World Cup was on and it seemed that England might have been in with a chance, the commis chef's visit to a tattoo parlour was made.

Whether it was due to light refreshment, which he said he had not consumed, that he did it I do not know. But the intended single tattoo on his arm with the words Beckham forever, became the partner for another tattoo and this one was in a more private area of his body. It was after a lot of persuasion that it was revealed. Now I must confess that in the light of a full moon or in this case a flickering faulty fluorescent light fitting it did have a certain attraction. This was the unanimous decision of the kitchen and waiting staff.

The young chef is now working as many hours as he can to save up the money to have Mr. Beckham's tattoo removed, so after all that the World Cup did do me a favour. It was good to see union flags and bunting outside local businesses many for the Queen's Jubilee and others for the football. However it was sad to see that as soon as England was out of the World Cup many of the flags came down.

I like to fly the union flag from the restaurant all the year round - and I like others had it flying upside down. Slap my wrists. A very kind gentleman who rang the restaurant on a Saturday night brought this to my attention. Thus with only fifteen minutes before forty-five covers would be arriving; with sauces still to be made and a desperate attempt in progress to cool down the potatoes for the brown shrimp dumplings; also a stuffing needed to be made for the pork fillets and I was informed that the flag was upside down. It's the sign of a ship in distress I was told. It was at that point the sweet pepper sauce boiled over, and thoughts of abandoning ship were in the back of my mind. Maybe on this occasion the flag was flying correctly.

This is a little dish that we would prepare for the sweet trolley in 1966. There was something else that happened that year, but for the life of me I can't remember what. .

Oranges in Caramel serves four

In the summer when the B B Q season is in full swing and there are lots of fresh salads I would offer a simple dessert that provides a refreshing end to a meal, Oranges in Caramel. A trolley terror from the 60s if ever there was one, a collection of badly trimmed slices, pith included, laying in sticky syrup. However if you take time to peel the fruit carefully and make a proper caramel the result is a revelation, and a good slosh of Grand Marnier does not go amiss.

8 medium size oranges 150 ml cold water 225g caster sugar 150ml very hot water

Peel the rind without the pith from four of the oranges and cut it in to very thin strips. Blanch them in a small pan of boiling water and after a few minutes drain the blanched peel, rinse with cold water and set aside.

Peel all the oranges to the flesh, over a bowl to catch the juices. Put the sugar and cold water in a medium size saucepan over a low flame shaking the pan as the sugar dissolves. Raise the heat and boil rapidly, until the syrup turns to a rich amber colour.

Remove the pan from the heat, cover your hands with a tea towel and slowly pour in the very hot water. Stir the caramel with a wooden spoon until it is thoroughly blended. If it is lumpy return the caramel back to the heat.

Add the orange zest to the syrup at this stage. Put your oranges in a bowl and pour the caramel over them. When they've cooled, place them in the fridge to chill. Serve with ice cream.

COR AIN'T IT HOT CHEF.

The metal chains that hang from the back door of the kitchen, designed to keep out the flies, were pushed apart and in came Mr. H the butcher. In his arms was the supply of meat for the restaurant for that day.
"Cor, it ain't half hot in this kitchen." " Is it?" I replied, "I don't think it's too bad."

His visit was quickly followed by Coles the fish monger, pushing his way through the chains as if it was a personal thing between man and the dreadful construction of fifty loose hanging chains. Once he and his box of sea bass, sea trout, and the half ton of samphire was fully safe in the kitchen, the long awaited words came out. "Cor, it ain't half hot in here!" "It's not too bad." I replied.

After he had departed in his van with air conditioning and all the mod cons, I slowly turned to the commis chef. You remember the one, now famous for his tattoos, looked him in the eyes and said "Is it hot in here?" "Well chef," he gasped to reply, "it's a bit warm, don't you think?" "Well lad you may be right, just a little bit warm, just a tad warm." It was then I went down one of my memory lane trips.

Warm you say? I will tell you what's warm. You should have worked in the kitchen when I first started, with a full kitchen brigade of ten chefs all working over an old coal fired oven. The long oven that was along one side of the kitchen was known as the black monster. It was one man's job through out the day to see that this fire-spitting monster was working to full power and woe betide him if the heat dropped when service was on. Many a time the head chef shouted at the top of his voice "Victor!" and Victor would come running with a long steel poker in his hand and, under the threat of death, he would bring the black monster back to its full power. Life in those days offered very different cuisine to the food we offer today; especially if you dined in the 50s and 60s hotel dining rooms.

It was in the days when it was edged in stone that cabbage had to be cooked for three hours. We all knew, as commis chefs, that the correct colour, if you wanted perfection with cabbage, was that of an old army ground sheet. Thank goodness the 1960s recipe for hotel cabbage has been lost in the pages of time, although a few chefs still seem to have a copy. One of my jobs was, each day, to make two fresh soups, and with a good supply of chicken bones, cream of chicken was a soup that was easy to make. Another soup that could be made quickly if you were in a hurry was Crème du Barry, a soup made from cauliflower.

Soups in the 50s were spoiled by the reputation of the soup called Brown Windsor and only the British could come up with a name that instantly puts you off wanting it. Seemingly made from wallpaper paste and gravy browning, it had the whiff of old bones and a pinky brown tint of stage make up. But as we all know a real fresh homemade soup can be a pleasure to eat and with that in mind I have a recipe for....

Homemade Tomato Soup

50g butter
2 med onions peeled and finely chopped
2 celery slicks finely diced
2 cloves of garlic finely chopped
700 g of ripe tomatoes skinned and chopped
pinch of sugar, salt, pepper,

750ml of a chicken or vegetable stock
5 to 6 basil leaves
125ml of fresh cream

Heat the butter in a good size saucepan, put in the chopped onions and add the celery allowing about 20 minutes for these to cook through. Add the chopped garlic and put into the pan the skinned and chopped tomatoes followed by the salt pepper and sugar. A word of warning - don't add too much of the seasoning at this stage as you can always add more later on. Now you can add the stock and the basil leaves.

Cook for 15 minutes over a good heat giving it a stir now and then. Remove the basil leaves and gently put into the liquidizer and then back into a clean pan. Stir in the fresh cream and gently reheat taking care not to let the soup boil. Taste and adjust the seasoning. Serve with fresh bread.

Conservatory at Rushmore's Restaurant

PREPARING THE RESTAURANT
FOR OPENING.

Would you Adam and Eve it? The month of October is the anniversary of Rushmore's restaurant's opening in Heacham. The time has just flown by. I remember when we first looked at the restaurant, thinking that pink must have been the in colour. The restaurant was pink, the bar was pink, and the conservatory was pink.

It was on a day in September, when I had a meeting with Sid. He was the gaffer of the company that was picked to redecorate the restaurant. We stood in the middle of the dining area, and he looked around. Slowly his hand came up to his chin, and then the words of wisdom came out.   " Green! That's the colour, with a nice pastel shade of corn flower for the top." " What about pink?" I replied. It was at that stage that Sid's bottom lip started to quiver and by the look on his face he gave me the answer. We shook hands and Sid departed. Over the next few weeks it was all hands on deck to prepare the restaurant for the planned opening date of 16th October. The restaurant had been closed for eighteen months, so there was a lot to do. It was always my intention to use as many local suppliers as possible, and to use fresh ingredients. As we wished to change the menu four or five times a year, with the seasons; it was important that our suppliers could provide us with local produce as far as possible. Shell fish from Brancaster, crabs from Cromer, meat that is from local farms, and bread baked fresh each day - that's the restaurants policy and we're sticking to it. All seemed to be coming along fine.

Sid and his team of decorators were doing battle with the pink. They all seemed to be in good moods and many a rendition of Lily the Pink was heard coming endlessly from the restaurant.

It was on a bright September day that I decided to buy Sid and his men a fish and chip lunch. As I entered the chip shop next door to the restaurant, known then as Pam's Plaice, I was greeted with, " Hello. This is Gordon and I am Pam." After the formalities were over, Pam asked if we would be offering fish and chips on my menu. "Not as I know, Pam" I replied. "Maybe we can come to a little arrangement. I wont sell fish and chips if you don't sell Tournedos Rossini." This arrangement seems to work for both of us and as Pam said, as I went out of the door, the sauce from the Rossini would leak through the paper bags.

Sid and mates enjoyed the fish and chip lunch, and as I had brought them the lunch they promised me that there would be no more renditions of Lily the Pink. Well at least not until tomorrow!

In early October having recruited the entire front of the house staff, I noted that according to my diary, I was to interview a young lad for the position of commis chef. I have, over many years, taken on lads and trained them up only for them to fly the nest. Like homing pigeons they head straight for London. The young man got the job as the commis chef and I am training him, so one day he too may be tempted to fly the nest and head for the bright lights of the city.

It was a sad day when Sid and all the workmen left. Then with all the tables with the linen on, large sparkling wine glasses and crisp white napkins, the restaurant was ready to open. As I stood there alone thinking of all the hard work that had been done, I thought that I could just make out the tune that two passing boys were singing, no it couldn't be…not Lily the Pink. I am pleased to say it wasn't.

I was pleased to receive a call from London. Dan, one of the many young chefs that started with me years ago, was coming to Norfolk. As he had to be back in London on the Monday it was arranged that we would meet at the restaurant on the Sunday. As Dan arrived he was introduced to all the staff and it was not long before the head chef from a well-known restaurant in London had sprung up a conversation with my commis chef. They reminded me of two pigeons. There was a lot of nodding going on and all with me trying to listen and cook at the same time. "How is Andrew?" I asked. He was another of my young chefs that had flown the nest to London many years ago. Dan replied that he was ok, working as a consultant for Canary Wharf, on mega bucks. All this talk of big money seemed to bring a sparkle to my commis chef's eyes and it has given him a renewed surge of enthusiasm. With all this big money chat, going on I said "Sorry lads, things to do. I can't stay here all day chatting I must push on… I am off to give a few grannies a good bashing."

View from Heacham South Beach bridge
where we caught the dabs

Granny Smiths Dessert Sorbet

The recipe will serve six persons. Roughly chop five or six granny smith apples, (you can leave the skin as this gives the sorbet a rich green colour) pop into a clean bowl and add 170g of white sugar. Pour over about half a cup full of sweet cider, and if you have it pour in a tot of brandy. Add the juice of two lemons and with clean hands mix all the ingredients together.

This is the important part. Pop the apple mix into your blender and blend the apples for 15 minutes. It seems a long time but you need to bring the apple mix to a pulp. Remove from the blender and put the mix through a fine mesh sieve, pushing it through with a spoon to get all the juices out. Find a container with a good fitting lid, and into this pour your strained apple. Then pop it into the deep freeze. After an hour remove from the freezer and with a fork give your sorbet a stir. The sorbet will require stirring every hour or so until it freezes.

This a recipe I tried a few weeks ago and its now on our restaurant menu served with honeydew melon as a starter. I felt that I had to share this recipe with you as it is easy to make, and when you taste it, it's a bombshell of flavours… a minefield of memories of apple orchards and sunny days. It's a Lily the Pink type of dish

GRANDFATHER'S CHRISTMAS TRIFLE.

When you see Easter eggs in the shops, and fireworks being let off since late July, Christmas day is not far away. The special day was always spent at my other grandmother's house that was about two miles from our home. As the magic hour of ten o'clock came it was time to walk the two miles to our grandmother's house. This walk seemed, as very small children, an effort but with the continual reminding that 'its not far now' coming from my father. Being a tall man his one stride was at least four steps for my sister and myself; but with the thought of the many presents that lay in wait we struggled to keep up.

Christmas day lunch was a sight to see, two fat capons, sage and onion stuffing, fluffy roast potatoes, and not to be missed Brussels sprouts all served in terrines with the gravy was in a sauceboat. One of the things that have stuck in my memories was that we always said grace on this special day, then Grandfather would carve the fowl, then slowly sitting down on his chair. He didn't say much, he didn't have to, his smiles to my sister and myself said it all. After the main course had been cleared, it was time for the long awaited pudding. This had being steaming in the old copper in the kitchen for the last few hours, and was brought to the table by a grandfather who had seen more Christmas puddings than he wished to remember. The pudding was never set alight and the little bottle of brandy brought to put into the brandy sauce, had been consumed long before Christmas day. Maybe at that early age in my life, my love of fine foods was giving me hassle because also on the table was a large bowl containing trifle, full to the brim and topped with fresh cream. I am sorry to say each year that we went to grandfathers for Christmas I never tried that trifle. Often on a crisp winters day when the wind is in the east I can, with the help of a game dealers chopping board, still start off the memories of Christmas past. The old Welsh dresser, tins of old oak ham, coal fires, and grandmothers mince pies, Christmas cake in an old Smiths Crisp tin, and last but not least the unforgettable grandfather's Christmas trifle.

Grandfather's Christmas Trifle

200ml whipping cream
200 ml milk
Half a vanilla pod split lengthways
12 amoretti biscuits or 160g of macaroons
5 tbsp sweet sherry
1 tbsp of brandy
4 tbsp good strawberry jam slightly warmed
4 egg yolks, 1 egg, 1 good tbsp caster sugar
275ml double cream
1 tbsp icing sugar
Angelica and silver balls to decorate

Every one loves a real home made trifle, the layers of the trifle may invoke an argument, but a real trifle should be composed of home made custard, good quality jam and lightly sweetened whipped cream. Putting jelly into a trifle is an abomination and also fresh fruit is often far too tart and somehow alien to the confection.

The quality of the custard is the most important layer of all. It must be made with eggs, vanilla, sugar, and cream and be thick enough to set in a layer. Another no, no, is to finish the trifle off with glace cherries and hundreds and thousands. Please just use angelica and silver balls. This is the classic trifle.

Scald the whipping cream and milk with the vanilla pod. Cover the pan to infuse. Lay the biscuits in a nice glass bowl and pour over the sherry and brandy and leave to soak, next spoon over the warmed jam.

Beat the egg yolks and the whole egg with the sugar in a bowl and strain the vanilla flavoured cream over the eggs. Mix together. Pour back into the cream pan and cook very gently over a low heat. Be very careful not to over cook, however the custard must be cooked enough to set. When you feel that the custard is ready strain over the soaked biscuits.

When cooled, put the bowl in the fridge for at least four hours or over night. Whip the double cream until it just holds its peaks and pile on top of the custard in a swirly way and decorate with the angelica and silver balls. Chill once more until ready to eat.

THE AA INSPECTOR CALLS

Over the many weeks leading up to Christmas I have always left a trail of hints for presents that Mrs. R. could buy me. Little things like a new fishing rod or any item that would increase my sparse so called collection of ageing fishing gear. Like many others I always imagine that I know what I am going to get. But then when I am given my present on Christmas day: don't you just know it; no way will a thirteen-foot fishing rod fit into a six inch by three-inch box. Slowly pulling the paper off I wonder if maybe, just maybe some clever dick has invented a fishing rod that would fit into a tiny box.

Over the first year in Rushmore's I applied to the AA for them to inspect the restaurant. In return we had a letter back confirming the menu was of AA rosette standard and stating we were to expect a visit when an inspector was in the area.

Now that was months ago. It was on a Thursday night many weeks ago when Kim was on duty in the restaurant, that she came in to the kitchen. I could see by the expression on her face that she had something to tell me. In the restaurant was a lady on her own. Instantly my thoughts were, was she the inspector from the AA? Kim went off to take her order, and when the order arrived in the kitchen it was as follows: Terrine of duck pate garnished with Cumberland sauce, and mixed leaves, followed by slow cooked fillets of English lamb in rosemary and red wine sauce. Also a half bottle of fine red wine was ordered.

As the starter plate arrived back from the restaurant, a close inspection of what was left on it took place. Nods of approval came from the commis chef, not much left, just a few bits of mixed leaves left on the plate.

When the main course left the kitchen we waited; after what seemed a life time the plate arrived back, just a little of the rosemary and red wine sauce was left. Smiles all round we thought that we had cracked it. Then, like me expecting a fishing rod to be in a small box, it turned out that the lady was staying in Heacham at a friend's holiday house for a few days rest.

Thinking one thing and it turning out to be the unexpected reminds me of a story that involved a rich landowner. A few years ago he had his head gardener plant asparagus. Each year, as soon as the first heads of asparagus had broken through the earth's crust, an under gardener would be sent at great haste up to the big house to inform his lordship.

It was on a bright sunny day that the head gardener, on his morning inspection, spotted a spear of asparagus of some size emerging. Like the wind, he ran up to the house to tell his master.

The master and the entire household promptly turned out to see this one marvellous spear of asparagus. The news was found to be neither false nor exaggerated. The plant had broken the ground. The head of it was round and shiny and mottled and gave promise of a column too thick to be encircled by the hand. There were cries of admiration at the sight of the horticultural phenomenon. As the days went by the master and the entire household would inspect the asparagus and each day it grew bigger, bigger than any asparagus had ever grown before. A special cutting knife was made by the local blacksmith and sharpened to slice the phenomenon with one swipe.

The great day arrived. His lordship had invited many of his friends and he made sure that the entire household would be there. His lordship advanced armed with the official instrument in hand and bent down with dignity to set about separating the proud plant from its stem. For a while everybody waited impatiently to examine the asparagus, but to their surprise, disappointment and dismay, his lordship rose up slowly empty handed.

The 'asparagus' was made of wood. The joke, which perhaps went a little too far, was the work of a young wood carver. He had fashioned the fake plant to perfection, buried it secretly and raised it little by little each day to imitate the process of natural growth. It turned out that the young man had tried to sell his lordship one of his woodcarvings a few years ago but was refused.

His lordship scarcely knew how to take this hoax but on seeing signs of hilarity on all present and this followed by great laughter, he held the wooden asparagus aloft, and laughed till tears rolled down his checks.

The evidence was accordingly taken away and for one evening at least the asparagus statue was granted the honour of the drawing room table. So with all these tales of slight disappointment I offer a few tips to make Christmas day lunch go without a hitch.

Cranberry sauce

This is easy and quick to make, prepare it in advance and store it in a covered container in the fridge for up to a week. Place 250g of fresh cranberries in a small saucepan with 150ml of water and bring gently to the boil. Reduce the heat and simmer for 5 minutes. Next add a few strips of orange peel and 100g of brown sugar. Stir to dissolve the sugar and simmer for a further 7 to 10 minutes until the sauce is thickened and pulpy. Now remove the orange slices and transfer the sauce to a small bowl. The cranberry sauce is now ready.

Classic Bread Sauce

This accompaniment is essential; serve with any game, chicken or turkey. Heat 600ml of milk in a small saucepan with 50g of butter, add into the pan a small skinned onion that has been studded with 5 or 6 whole cloves, pop in a bay leaf if you have one and also a few sprigs of thyme would not go amiss.

Bring this up to the boil and then reduce the heat and just simmer for 15 minutes. Strain the flavoured milk into another pan, stir in 100g of fresh white bread crumbs and simmer again for 4 minutes over a low heat until thickened, lastly add 3 to 4 tbsp of single cream. Season the sauce with salt and pepper and grated nutmeg. Don't be tempted to make this sauce too early in the day as it will become too thick and loose its light texture.

FAILED RESOLUTIONS

I know what Victor Meldrew would have said; I don't believe it. In a previous story, I wrote about my ageing fishing gear. Well my old faithful rods and odds and sods that only fishermen collect; the very items that have been my passport to the great escape, at least for a few hours, have gone. It was by a chance glance at the garage door that I saw that all was not well. I could not have missed it.

Maybe it was the fact that the garage door was merrily swinging in the wind and on closer inspection it was even clearer to me, as the round thing I was standing on was the old brass handle that had been ripped from the garage door. It was then that I felt that 'I don't believe it; Meldrew' seemed to have taken me over. I headed straight indoors to report the crime to Mrs R. With a strong cup of coffee inside me, it dawned on me that things maybe were not as bad as they seemed. The contents were well insured, and in the words of Mr Woo, it's turned out fine again.

After the fourth cup of coffee and as it was a new year I thought that I would have a go at making and keeping a few New Year resolutions. How about giving up my old trusty pipe? Me and my pipe go back a long time. I was the only boy caught smoking a pipe behind the bike sheds. The teacher that caught me and three other boys told us that he could smell the scent of golden rough-cut shag 200 yards away.

How about cutting my working week down to say, two days a week. The bank manager I believe would pooh pooh that idea. The more I began to think about these simple New Year resolutions, which I could take on board, the longer the list became. Then it came to me; no need to go silly.

How about all the little things that send Mrs R into orbit: things like putting the toilet seat down after use, putting my razor back in its little plastic holder, and then there is the soap on the hand basin. Will you please put both socks in the laundry bin as you now have a drawer full of odd socks? I am sure that somewhere in the house is a great mountain of odd socks just waiting to be reunited.

Beer cans, that's another sore point. What's that green box for? What green box? With the thoughts of the stolen fishing gear in the back of my mind, I was ready to give it my full shot on this New Year's resolutions malarkey. All was well for a few days but then it had to happen. Who left the toilet seat up?? It didn't take long to work that one out as there was only Mrs R and me in the house. Damn silly thinking that things like toilet seats left up, razors left on the side of the sink, beer cans not put into the correct colour green box could ever be eradicated. It's part of life. But by way of apology, as I had a few days off, I decided to give Mrs R a treat with a special meal.

Fillet of Pork Wellington
With a fresh sage cream sauce

A classical dish, just the job for a birthday treat or dinner party and one of many dishes on my new restaurant menu. What's required for two persons? Ask your butcher for a pork fillet or it can be called pork tenderloin. Ask him to remove any of the fine skin from the outside of the pork fillet and make sure the size will be enough for two persons.

Season the fillet of pork with a little salt and if you have it freshly grated black pepper. Leave the pork in one piece and pop onto a baking tray. Drizzle a little oil on to the meat and place it into a preheated medium hot oven. Cooking time will be around 15/20 minutes; the pork wants only to be pink. Remove from the oven, and leave to cool.

You will require a small pack of shop bought puff pastry thawed out. Roll the pastry out on a floured table. The pastry needs to be thin. Take the cooled pork and place in the middle of the pastry. With the yolk of only one egg, brush egg round the outside of the pastry to form a seal; gently fold the pastry round the pork so it looks like a large sausage roll. With the rest of the egg, glaze the pastry ready for the oven.

Place the pastry filled with pork into a medium hot oven for say, 15 minutes, but a word of warning, with the pork inside cooked already, you are only cooking the pastry to a rich golden crispy brown. Keep an eye on it.

Next for the sauce, take a small pan, pop a little olive oil, say two tablespoons full, in your pan and add around half of a very finely chopped white onion, followed by chopped fresh sage approx two table spoons. Leave for a tick over the heat for the onion to slowly cook out. Add, if you have a little, around half a glass of dry white wine and allow it to reduce. After the sauce has reduced down to half add the fresh cream, say a very good splash or two.

Turn the heat down to a very gentle heat and allow the cream, wine, onions and fresh sage to infuse. By this time the pork should be ready. Place the pork in pastry on a chopping board, take a very sharp knife and slice the Wellington, arrange on good size plates, and pour with care the sage sauce around the pork.

EATING ON THE HOOF

On one of our days off we often spend the morning shopping in King's Lynn, and it was on one of these days that Mrs. R and myself spent a few hours in the town. I can't be doing with all that in and out of endless shops; she said 'I must just pop in here, wont be long', leaving me to stand out side. Half an hour later, yes you've guessed it, I am still waiting.

The time I spent out side was not wasted for I am a great people watcher, and I was amazed at the amount of people that I saw eating on the hoof. Many of those consuming their lunch were smartly dressed office and shop workers taking their lunch break. Others were young persons, casually walking along eating, a top up of their daily requirements. In the States over, what we now call, 'the pond' eating food in this manner is on a very much larger scale. In New York it is said that many tons of hamburgers are popped away each day. For the consumption of the hamburger the body must be upright and the legs moving.

The coordination of this art of eating can be a risky habit if you are crossing a busy main road. Maybe that's why you often see half eaten hamburgers, and hotdogs laying in the gutter. The craving for a form of spicy food in a bread based covering seems to be on the increase, but is it something new I ask myself. As one of the characters from the vicar of Dibley would have said, 'no, no, no, no, of course its not.'

It's the jolly old Romans that we can blame, or at least for part of it, a concoction of dough with a spicy topping known as the pizza. The most basic pizzas are thought to have been cooked on hot flat stones, and it was not until a 1000 years ago that the herb covered circles of dough became popular in Naples.

Foccacia, as it was known then, was served up as a snack, maybe to be eaten on the hoof. Dough was pounded into a thin crust and baked with leftovers as a topping. It was peasant food, and like the hamburger you did not need any utensils to eat it.

What we now know as the pizza of today would not have existed without some old world Europeans that conquered their great fear of the tomato, which was thought to be very poisonous. The tomato was brought to Europe from Peru and Ecuador in the 1500s and it was not regarded safe to eat until the late 1600s.

By the 18th century, street vendors in Naples were selling pizzas, and would you believe it the world's first pizzeria opened in 1890. The pizza soon became a big hit, so much so that around 1889 Queen Margherita of Italy asked a tavern owner to make a special pizza for her and being the very clever and cunning chap that he was he named the pizza in her honour. It was about the same time that Mozzarella, red tomatoes, and green basil were used, the colours of the Italian flag. The pizza, before long, travelled beyond the shores of the homeland and with it the secret came to USA. This being a country with many Italian immigrants it made many a poor man a large fortune. The first pizzeria opened in the States in 1905, in New York Cities Spring Street, and its said that you can still dine there today.

It was in the 1950s that the commercial value of the pizza was exploited and with it the birth of the pizza hut and other chains that ensured the market was worldwide. The thin crust pizza I can take or leave, but a Texan gentleman living in Chicago, by the name of Ike Sewell, is said to have invented my favourite, the deep pan pizza. So there you have it, food that can be eaten on the hoof, has been around for a long time. Maybe people in Rome at the time moaned about all the old pizza crusts laying in the gutters. In the early 1980s we owned the restaurant La Casa and it was there that I employed a chef that could cook a deep pan pizza that you would die for. So for all us people that prefer not to eat on the hoof, I offer you his recipe for Deep Pan Pizza.

Deep Pan Pizza

A great pizza is not just a load of soggy, stringy, cheese on a base of dough enriched with ingredients that should never have been put together. It's the old, old story what goes in is what comes out. Good ingredients, love and time will make a good deep pan pizza. So let's make a start.

First of all we must consider the sauce that will cover the pizza's dough base. This sauce is a rich tomato sauce, and to make it take a medium size saucepan with a thick bottom, add a few drops of good quality olive oil and to this add one medium size fine chopped onion. Next into the pan chopped tomatoes, in the summer time I normally would use very ripe plum tomatoes but at other times of year I prefer to use a medium size tin of chopped tomatoes brought from your local shop. If you find that there is not sufficient juice in the tomatoes then add a little white wine or water. So now we have the oil, chopped onion and tomatoes in the pan. Next turn on the heat on the top of the cooker and pop the saucepan over a gentle heat. Once the sauce starts to cook add a clove of crushed garlic and, most important, a must is the herb oregano. If you use a dried form of oregano, a couple of good pinches are then stirred into the sauce. The sauce will require a gentle heat until the onion and tomatoes have formed a rich sauce. On a slow heat this will take an hour or so to reduce. Once this has been done, allow the sauce to cool down and add the seasoning, salt and pepper, to your taste.

Next we will need to make the pizza base. It's up to you. You can go to the trouble of making your own, but why not ask your local baker if they will sell you one pound of basic bread dough in a plastic bag. To keep the dough for a few days pop it in a fridge. It will slowly rise in the fridge but you can knock it back. OK on we go, next take a deep sandwich tin around 9inches. This size will feed two persons. Grease it very lightly, take your bread dough and knock it back and roll out to fit the tin but with surplus dough to mould up the side of the tin. The pizza crust wants to be half an inch thick.

Spoon the cooled tomato sauce over the bread base. The oven should have been switched on by now at a hot heat, so it is ready to accept the almost finished pizza. Now for the toppings. I use only ingredients that go well together; grated cheese, sliced tomatoes, and maybe a slight hint of onion.

These should be thinly sliced and placed on the pizza in the following order, the grated cheese (I like to use plain cheddar cheese) then the sliced tomatoes, then if you wish a little very fine sliced onion and a pinch of oregano to complete. Bake in a good hot oven, check after say 10 minutes. The pizza should start to rise up allowing the rich sauce to soak into the bread base.

As the pizza bakes you must allow for the thicker base to cook, you should finish up with a deep pan pizza. Once out of the oven serve the pizza with a good fresh salad and maybe a jacket potato, but what ever you do please lock all the doors, for the last thing we want is for somebody to take a slice and walk down the Street and be seen eating it on the hoof.

MY TEENAGE YEARS

There is an old saying; if you can remember the 60s then you weren't there. It was that time of my life that was pure magic, and like many others of that time I was a teenager in love. It was the years of the mini skirt, knee length boots, and the famous beehive hairstyle, polo neck sweaters, and the DA hair cut. We had a coffee bar in town called the Whiskey-a-Go-Go. It was a place that was packed to the rafters with teenagers sipping their frothy coffee or a bottle of coke, and of course, the jukebox was playing the top tunes of the day, simple pleasures. Sadly the Whiskey a Go Go has long gone but I can still see that coffee bar in my mind and the sounds of 'Sweets for my Sweet' coming from the juke box when I walk pass that area of town.

Also you could see all the top groups at the time at the local dance hall with a support band on a Saturday night for ten bob, a skin full of Red Barrel, followed by a fish and chip supper and still have change out of a pound note, happy times. The old saying about the swinging sixties was I suppose related to the flower power hippy brigade, with most of them living in cloud cuckoo land. All that puffing and popping must have given inspiration to many of them as they performed their individual type of ritual dancing. I often wonder when I see a girl in a little world of her own dancing around her handbag if this is a throw back to those hippy days.

It was in the early sixties and I had just started work at a large hotel as a commis chef. Just across the market square was the town's dance hall and on each Saturday night we had one of the many up and coming groups performing on stage at the hall. The Swinging Blue Jeans, Johnny Kidd and the Pirates, The Bachelors, The Animals, with their hit 'House of the

Rising Sun', Eden Kane, and loads more such as the Barron Knights and the Rocking Berries. But I suppose the one that caused a real stir was Mr. P. J Proby, as all those that went to see him witnessed him finish his act by splitting his pants on stage. It was only a few days ago that I was telling a retired police inspector about those nights and he said that at the time he was one of the bobbies on the beat that had to escort Mr. Proby back to the hotel due to the fans that came to see him.

My personal involvement in a band lasted for two years. I was the drummer for the Countdowns, a local band. We were once asked to be the supporting group for the Shadows, but the hours that I spent in the kitchens had to come first, happy times.

Often if the groups were not travelling back to London, they would stay in the hotel over night and as a young commis chef that was always on the early breakfast shift, it was often possible, with the help of a nod from the hall porter, to be in the right place at the right time. On one occasion after I had finished cooking breakfast, the head waiter said " you are requested in the restaurant, that over paid groupie lot wants to thank you for their breakfast." That groupie lot as he had described them was not in Frank's, the headwaiter's, top ten. Vera Lyn might have been but not the Barron Knights as it turned out to be.

In those days on a Saturday night and after the dance hall had closed we all headed off to a fish and chip shop in the town. This was the place that all the local groups met and you always knew which groups were in already because the street would be littered with old vans and cars full of drums and equipment. By the early hours the place was heaving as it had a very good reputation for its fry-ups.

As you entered the premises you were led into an area at the back, and laid out in three small rooms was an arrangement of odd tables and chairs. The tables were covered with plastic table cloths that could easily be cleaned and so quickly relaying the tables for the next punters that were waiting to enjoy a fry up in the early hours of the morning.

The menu was simple you started with chips, and added to this any item that could be fried in oil. Old oval plates were used to convey the delight of this fry up and I suppose after a few pints of Red Barrel it seemed a very welcoming sight. One trick that we soon learnt from those that had been to this to establishment many times before was to ask for a dessertspoon as your meal arrived. This was not so you could eat your mushy peas with out dropping them on the lino, no you slid the spoon under your plate so that all the excess oil ran down to one end of the plate. It was, I suppose, our little contribution to healthy eating.

I suppose now after forty odd years have past, the magic of being a teenager in the sixties has never gone away. It was the music, the dress and hairstyles that gave that time of my life so many happy memories. Over the last few years I have met and become friends with a few of the legends of that era. One that is top of my list is Joe Brown and, when he did a summer season in Norfolk, my wife and I went out to dinner on many occasions with Joe and the Bruvvers. Going out to dinner we always seemed to finish up at the only place that would feed us at the unearthly hour of almost midnight, the local Indian restaurant.

Long gone are the plates of greasy fry ups, but in their place spicy concoctions of chicken in a mouth burning curry sauce, washed down with not Red Barrel but Tiger beer; that at least if drunk in large quantities will help in cooling down the mind blowing chilli and lime concoction that Joe seemed to like and made sure that you at least tried. This always seemed to bring a smile to his face as you reached for the Tiger beer.

It has long been a theory of mine that bands of the sixties that are still doing the circuits have had to adapt their eating habits as the years have passed them by, greasy egg chips and mushy peas have given way to spicy foods of many nations. The food may have changed but not the music and the memories. These Sixties groups are still playing a lot of the same tunes, because there will never be a substitute for the music of that magic era.

So if there is a knock on the door and on opening it you find an ageing pop star ask him in and grab the frying pan and some oil not for a greasy fry up of the Sixties but to fry up a spicy dish in the pan.

Spicy Chicken in a Pan

Take a frying pan of good size put this on the stove on a good heat. Add a drop of olive oil and when the oil is fairly hot add half a leek that has been sliced thinly, also add half of a large onion, again this must be thinly sliced. Take a red pepper, cut it in half and remove the seeds and again slice thinly and add to the pan.

It's best if all the ingredients are prepared before hand. Once the leek, onion and pepper is in the pan stir them gently so they all start to cook at the same time. It's now time to add your chicken, which must be very finely sliced and once in the pan must be stirred. Now for the spicy bit; when you feel that the chicken is cooked add a good pinch of paprika and stir well in and to this you add fresh cream to make the sauce. Season with salt and pepper to your taste. The spicy chicken in paprika should be served on a plate of hot long grain rice. The best way to serve this meal is to turn the lights down low, crank up the gramophone and pop on an old 45.

**Colin in his Restaurant in Heacham
A long time after his Teenage Years!**

MORE MEMORIES OF TEENAGE YEARS

It was a chance remark that my father made back in the 1950's when I was a slip of a lad and long before the urge to make a mess and create classical dishes in my mother's kitchen. Size is not every thing was the off the cuff remark, and to this day I haven't a clue why he came out with it. We were at the time in the garden. Not a garden as described in any dictionary, that is a place that flowers grew; not for my old dad, the word garden in dad's dictionary was described as fifty square feet of solid concrete and the most important gardening tool was the stiff yard brush. I at this tender age had never met anybody else with a dislike of anything to do with gardening. After a lot of thought, maybe the remark was regarding the size of the yard brush that father had put me in sole charge of. Well that's what I hoped he was referring to.

Anyway "size is not every thing" was firmly embedded in the back of mind. In my early days of courting young ladies, size is not every thing once again reared its ugly head. This time it was not said by my dear old dad but by a young lady that I was sweet on at the time.

I decided to cook her an intimate meal for two. In conversation I had found out that she liked shellfish so I decided that the starter would be mussels cooked in white wine and cream sauce. I had planned on oysters but a commis chef's wages would not stretch to such items even if the old tales of the oysters were true.

All was going great, the mussels were consumed, and in time I headed off into the kitchen for the grand presentation of the main course. The main course was to be a simple little dish that had been determined by the change left over from buying the mussels, white wine and half a pint of cream. It was, that classical dish and favourite of all young ladies, Toad in the Hole. Unknown to me the young lady had followed me into the kitchen and as I bent over to remove my concoction of lightly raised Yorkshire pudding filled with perfectly cooked pork sausages, she stopped me in my tracks with, let me do that for you.

Maybe it was the effect of the mussels, I didn't stop to ask as there for all to see was a complete failure. My toads were black as your hat and as for something that could only loosely be described as Yorkshire pudding: it was as flat as a pancake. Then the fearful and long awaited words came out, size is not everything. There was not much conversation as we tried to consume toad in the hole that tasted as bad as it looked. Needless to say I never saw that young lady again.

Time has moved on and forty years have passed under the bridges of time, and in that time I have been experimenting on how to cook the perfect Yorkshire pudding. I know that many of you will have your own favoured recipes that may have been passed down from mother to daughter; but if you are a young lad of sixteen that's intending to cook toad in the hole as a special treat for a young lady, then here are a few tips that may be of help.

Number one: make the batter the night before in a plastic container and after whisking it for a few minutes with a large wire whisk to incorporate as much air as possible, cling film it and leave over night in a cool place, but not in the fridge. In the morning remove the cling film and gently whisk again for a minute. The oven that you are cooking your pudding in should be of a medium to high heat. You need this to start the pudding off. You can open the oven after a few minutes and look to see if the pudding is starting to rise and at that stage you can if you wish turn the heat down a little. But remember it still requires a good heat, and must only be cooked in an oven that contains no other foods.

One thing that I have found that makes a good Yorkshire, is the size of pudding tins that are used. You can buy those large tins that only contain four on a tray, but for perfection I have containers that are made of earthenware. The most important thing with these is that they are a good inch deep and this helps the pudding to rise. Another tip is to make sure that the fat you use in the tin is only added to the tin after you have pre-warmed the tins in the oven. Well I hope that these tips go a little way in helping some love sick young man cook a candlelight dinner for a young lady. At least if he follows these instructions he may have a chance of avoiding the immortal words: size is not everything. Even so if his Yorkshire did not rise to her expectations then he could offer the old Norfolk saying Small is Bootifull.

Forget the Yorkshire pudding and go for a dainty little dish that my commis chef Dan Addison says really works with the young ladies.

Smoked Salmon, Prawns and Cromer Crab

Smoked salmon, prawns and fresh Cromer crab; all of these ingredients can be bought from your local fishmonger or supermarket. You will require, depending on the amount of young ladies that you are entertaining, peeled prawns, (the small bag of frozen ones will do), a pack of smoked salmon, and the dressed crabs. Buy one crab for every two persons. You will also require a small amount of mayonnaise, a drop of tomato sauce, a lemon and one of those little bags of mixed salad leaves.

To plate up this dish, which can be served as a starter or with some small new potatoes as a main dish in the summer; there is just one other item you want to make this dish look stunning. You will need my secret weapon, a metal ring. These you can buy from any good cooks' shop.

Plating the dish up: take a large white plate and place around the edges the selection of mixed leaves. On to the plate you now place two or three slices of the smoked salmon. Next place the metal ring in the centre, and almost fill the ring with defrosted prawns that you have first mixed in a bowl together with a little mayonnaise and a dash of tomato sauce. Remove the flesh from the crabs' shell and gently mix together and spoon on top of the prawns and finish off by putting a blob of mayonnaise on the top of the crab. If you have a sprig of parsley then pop a bit on the top, it only remains to slice a wedge of lemon and with a gentle upward movement lift the metal ring off, and there you have it, I wish that I had known of this little dish forty odd years ago.

LATE NIGHT ENCOUNTER WITH MRS R.

My wife is always complaining that I do not listen to her. Well it had to happen, Mrs R. has gone over the top this time and shown her real colours. It all started after a very busy Saturday night in the restaurant. We had just arrived home.

I decided to sit in the kitchen and unwind and had just poured myself a cool beer and sat contemplating the busy Sunday lunch that was coming up. It was then I heard Mrs R. say something to me that I did not catch. "What was that you just said?" "You never listen do you?" She probably was right especially at almost two in the morning.

At last I got the jist of it. She was going into the other room to pop the telly on and check her lottery ticket. Then it happened, it sounded like a cross between a jet aircraft taking off and a female cat that was trying to escape from an old tomcat. The next thing I heard made me almost spill my beer. "YES, YES, I have six numbers up." Cor blimey, I heard that all right; six numbers well that's a small fortunes worth.

It was at that moment that my mind went into fantasyland. Forget having to travel miles to go fishing, I will have my own lake. Should it be the red or maybe the yellow sports car? What make should it be? How much money should we give to the family? It was just then that all seemed to go very quiet so I thought it was time to offer my congratulations to Mrs R. My thoughts recalled the last time that she had a small win on four numbers. It was made clear to me that it was her ticket and her winnings. Now we are not just looking at four numbers but six. I might have to prove that some of my hard earn cash may have been responsible for paying for the winning ticket, or failing that find myself a good solicitor.

As I started to say well done, Mrs R dropped her bomb shell, she briefly flashed the winning ticket in front of me, "yes I have got six winning numbers up but…." The word but, seemed to come across as a long drawn out word. I thought for a moment I'd soon hear the long awaited words "and you are not having any of it, its mine." Not so this time but, there it was that word again. Mrs R then informed me that her six winning numbers were in fact on two lines, and the grand total of the win was twenty pounds.

Slowly I decided to sit down. She seemed to have a look of satisfaction on her face, and then she said, "Work tomorrow, did you hear that??." All that was left for me was to contemplate one of my new recipes, and dream of another days work tomorrow.

Slow Cooked Lamb Fillets
on a Pea Mash with a Mint and Red Wine Sauce

This is a little dish that I created for my restaurant, and is still one of the best sellers. You will require two lamb fillets per person, and ask your butcher for best end fillets. The lamb has to be cooked very slowly in a gravy. To produce the gravy don't go to all the trouble that we do, you can cheat a little by using a powdered gravy mix.

So here we go: say for two people, make up about a pint of the gravy and bring to a light simmer, pour in a small glass of red wine and add a few sprigs of chopped fresh mint. Please note the gravy needs to be of a slightly thicker consistency that you would pour on your meat, and it should be cooked in a thick-bottomed saucepan.

Add the four lamb fillets to the sauce, and cook on a low heat for two hours just making sure that the fillets are not allowed to stick to the bottom of the pan. Now for the pea mash. Peel about four good size potatoes, cut into chunks and cook in lightly salted water. When the potatoes come up the boil, add a small packet of garden peas or if you wish you can add a can of mushy peas after you have mashed the potatoes. Either way you will finish up with the same basic pea mash. Stop confusing the recipe Rushmore. Back to the plot: just a little tip you can cook the mash hours before if you wish and reheat it in the oven with a knob of butter on top.

So the potatoes are cooked, drain off the water and add a small knob of butter and then mash the potato and pea mixture, add a little more seasoning if required. The lamb fillets do need the two hours slowly cooking to make them tender, if you find that the sauce is too thick add a little more red wine.

Presentation of the dish is as follows. Place a nice spoon full of the mash in the middle of the plate, place the two fillets gently on top, and spoon the sauce over and around the mash. If you wish place a little fresh mint on top of the lamb, serve with baby new season carrots, and buttered spring cabbage.

FAVOURITE RECIPES
FROM THE RESTAURANT

Pan Fried Chicken Livers

This dish is one of the most ordered starters in the restaurant. You will need around one pound of chicken livers if serving them for four persons.

Heat a large frying pan, add a good knob of butter and allow it to gently melt. Take the chicken livers and dust with seasoned flour then drop them into the melted butter and cook slowly for six to eight minutes. Just a note of warning: chicken livers for some reason tend to spit back as you cook them so be warned.

In the restaurant we serve them slightly pink, but you cook them as you wish. Once you feel that they are ready add to the pan half a glass of red wine and allow it to reduce down. It is then you will need a glass full of chicken stock and this must be added and reduced as well until a rich sauce has been made.

Take another frying pan add a spot of cooking oil to it, once heated cut out croutons of bread and fry to a golden brown. Then add slices of bacon and these, once cooked, will complete the dish by placing them on top of the warm livers.
To present the livers take a white plate, garnish with a few dressed mixed leaves around the edge and place the warm crouton of fried bread in the centre of the plate. Pile the livers on to the crouton and pour the sauce over. Lastly dust a little mixed herbs over if you have some, then add the bacon as a topping.

Pan Fried Wild Mushrooms

What a taste on a plate. Wild mushrooms served in a light white wine and cream sauce. To make the dish you will need a small amount of shop brought puff pastry. Roll this out thinly and cut a round shape with a wine glass, glaze with egg yolk and bake to a golden colour.

Next take a frying pan add a nice blob of real butter and when up to heat add your wild mushrooms. Once the mushrooms are in the hot butter they will only require a few minutes cooking. Fresh wild mushrooms are very tender, so use a wooden spoon to toss them around so that they cook through in the butter.

Once this has been achieved add a little dry white wine to the pan, then pour a spot of double cream in and gently mix together. Season with care.

Take the warm puff pastry case and with the aid of a sharp knife split the case in half. Place one of the slices of pastry on a plate, pile the wild mushrooms on top and then place the other pastry slice on top. Pour the sauce around the mushrooms and garnish with chopped parsley.

Smoked Trout Pate

Smoked trout when blended with butter will make a pate that will give you a simple starter that any fish lover will enjoy. It's one of those dishes that tastes better than anything that you will buy from the shops.

You need to buy a packet of smoked trout fillets. These are available from any good supermarket these days. Remove them from the packaging and look for any small fish bones these must be removed.

Plug in your blender and place the trout fillets, slightly flaked in the blender. Next take about the same weight of slightly softened butter, chop into small pieces and add that to the trout. You will also require the juice of almost half a lemon. The lemon juice can be added, at the end of the blending stage, in small amounts to season the trout pate and don't forget a pinch of salt and pepper to bring out all the flavours.

Switch on the blender on a slow speed to mix together the trout fillets and butter. As you see the trout and the butter blending into a smooth paste you can increase the speed of the blender. A word of warning: try not to over blend the pate as the mix may become too creamy and will have no body to it.

Once the trout pate has been blended and seasoned to your taste scoop the pate out of the blender and fill small ramekin dishes with the mix. As a starter you will not want to serve large amounts as the taste often lingers on the palate. Warm toast or lightly salted biscuits should be served with the pate and I always place a ramekin of good horseradish sauce on the table, as it goes well with any smoked fish.

Warm Tart With Cheese
And Poached Egg

This is one of those starters that on a very busy night is classed as a pain in the whatever. Not so much the dainty handmade tart that has been filled with cheese and cooked to perfection, but on a very busy dinner service poaching eggs to order can be a nightmare. Normally it seems once one warm tart topped with a poached egg goes out into the restaurant and the customers see it, then the orders come flooding in. Its like when you sell a sambucca you can put money on it, "What's that person drinking over there, waiter?" "Well sir, it's a glass of Italian stuff we serve it in a small glass with three hard coffee beans in it, then we set fire to it. Would you like one, sir?" "Yes please. Do you drink it alight waiter?" "Well you can if you wish sir, but please allow me to get you a very large glass of water if you are intending to do so, sir."

Although it's a hassle, if you are only required to serve a few for a dinner party then its not too bad. As a warm starter you cannot go wrong with this dish. The taste of a freshly made cheese tart topped with a warm poached egg is worth all the trouble. At the restaurant we have a number of small tins that we make the tarts in, they can be brought from any good cook shop.

Make up a savoury pastry and roll it out thinly so that you can line out the small tins. Having done this we use a cheddar cheese that has a bit of a bite to it. Fill the pastry lined tins with a good helping of cheese.

Crack two eggs into a small bowl and add a cup full of cream. This mix should fill six to eight tart cases. With a fork or whisk blend the eggs and cream together, season the blend with salt and pepper to taste.

Place the cheese filled cases on to a baking tray and gently pour or spoon the egg mixture into the cases. Preheat an oven to a medium heat and place the tray into the oven to cook.

The cooking time is about twenty minutes, but I would suggest that you check the tarts after fifteen minutes and you may have to turn the oven down slightly.

The tarts should be, if cooked correctly, golden brown on the top, as the egg mixture sets the melted cheese. Turn the oven down to the lowest point so that they keep warm.

A shallow saucepan or frying pan filled with water that has had a spoonful of vinegar in it must now be brought to the boil. Once boiling, crack your eggs into it and poach them so they are just set.

Remove the cheese filled cases from the warm oven and with the help of a table knife ease the pastry cases out of the tins and place on a warm plate. Decorate the plate with a few mixed leaves. Lift the cooked poached eggs out of the water with a slotted spoon and place on top of the tart. To make the dish work please do not over cook the poached egg it must be still soft so that when you cut into it the yolk runs and mixes with the cheese.

Prawn Pancake with Cheese Sauce

This is a dish that we used as a starter back in the days of my first restaurant in the early 1980's. The restaurant, as many will remember, was the one that I opened with my dear friend the late John Brundle, father of Martin Brundle from formula one racing fame.

As in those days like today we make the little pancakes all by hand. It's a starter that was on my first restaurant menu and you will still find it being offered on my menu today. It's a dish that has stood the test of time and is still a great favourite of many people just as it was over twenty years ago.

To make this dish you will require a frying pan that will not stick when making the pancakes. Also it only wants to be a small pan as this dish is very filling.

Make a batter with plain flour, eggs and milk, season it with salt and pepper and make sure that the batter is lump free. Heat up your pan on the stove so it gets very hot. Pop a small blob of butter into the pan. Next pour a little of the pancake batter into the hot pan. With your wrist move the pan from side to side to allow the batter to coat the bottom with a thin coat. Replace it on the heat to cook.

The pancake only requires a minute on each side. If you cook them any longer you can use them for soling your shoes. Once you have made the correct amount of pancakes, pile them on a plate and cover with a clean cloth.

White sauce is the next thing we will need. This is made by putting margarine or butter into a small saucepan and once melted add the same amount of flour. Mix together to form a roux and then slowly add warm milk stirring all the time with a whisk until you come up with a thick creamy white sauce. Season to taste with salt and pepper.

So now you have the pancakes and a white sauce. Prawns are what we want now, these can be frozen pawns that have been left to defrost, and once they are defrosted its time to put the dish together.

An oval white dish is what we at the restaurant serve our pancakes in. You know the ones. They are often used in restaurants to serve vegetables. Lay the pancake so that half of it is covering the bottom of the dish and add a good portion of the prawns, next add a few ounces of grated cheese over the prawns. Spoon over this a little of the white sauce, fold the rest of the pancake over and make sure that its all inside the dish. It now only requires a little more of the sauce to be added to cover the pancake before topping with more of the cheese. The pancakes can be made in the morning and kept in the fridge.

To bake the pancakes place them on a baking tray and place in a very hot oven. They will require fifteen to twenty minutes in a normal household oven. When cooked the hot pancake, still served in its dish that's laced with prawns and a creamy melted cheese sauce, should just need crusty warm bread to make a starter to remember.

Recipe for Crispy Batter

This is batter that we use all the time at the restaurant. It's ideal for cooking deep fried vegetables in, and can be used as a vegetarian dish served with spiced rice and laced with a sweet plum sauce, or deep frying pak choi that can be used as a bed for fillets of sea bass.

Take 1lb of self-raising flour and place it in a bowl, add a pinch of salt then into the centre of the flour put a good pinch of bicarbonate of soda. Pour two tablespoonfuls of malt vinegar over the bicarb. This will start to react and will gently froth up, slowly add cold water or if you have a spare bottle of lemonade you can use that. Work the mixture to a lump free batter with a whisk. Once you have your batter it will improve by placing it in the fridge for a few hours or it can be left over night and used the next day. Make sure that you give it a good stir before dipping your vegetables in the batter.

Pre cook and cool the vegetables that you wish to coat in the batter. Drain and dry the vegetables and dip into seasoned flour before popping them into the batter. Slowly remove them and gently drop into hot fat to cook.

As the crispy batter cooks they will need turning in the oil. Cooking time is only a few minutes. Once cooked, lift them out of the hot oil and drain on kitchen paper to remove any excess cooking oil. You should then finish up with crispy battered fried vegetables.

The Conservatory entrance inside which you can enjoy a pre meal drink or relax with a cup of coffee.

THE OUTSIDE CATERING LARK
(our in between years)

Outside catering has been around for at least 2000 years. There was this guy that had a beard and wore a long white smock, and on his first outside catering commission he was asked to do this big job on a hillside. He was to feed 5000 people on the day. Well he totally under estimated the food required for the job in hand and only turned up with five loaves and five fishes. The rest is history.

When in the 1980's I was running my first restaurant I was head hunted by the royal estate at nearby Sandringham. We were running a very busy restaurant at the time but to cut the story short, after a visit to Sandringham came away with a contract to supply 1000 meals a week on a cook/chill basis.

These 1000 meals had to be cooked, complete with all the vegetables, and delivered to their restaurant on the Royal Estate. This meant that once the chefs had finished cooking for the restaurant guests, we then had to start cooking for the Sandringham estate, and often finished at four in the morning.

With this contract under my belt I decided to sell the restaurant and set up a company called Colin Rushmore Cuisine.

We set up the operation in a 2000sq foot kitchen and placed adverts in the local newspapers.

The first job that we received was a function at our local town hall. At the time the kitchen was not ready so we cooked all the food in my garage on gas rings. The other problem was transport, as I had not bought the van. So on the Friday morning I went to see the local garage which had a large van for sale. On the pretence of a test drive, that would last at least two days, I had a van.

The outside catering lasted for 12 years. We went into most of the finest country houses in Norfolk as well as many of the village halls. Some of the latter left very much to be desired. Tables and chairs that you had to clean before you could use them. Facilities that could only be described in very loose terms as kitchens.

Over the 12 years many things happened as we worked this part of Norfolk. There was the day when we set off in good time to cater for a funeral at a house that was out in the sticks in marshland. As we entered the village we pulled up at the local pub and I asked the landlord if he knew where the house was. He had never heard of it, nor had any of the village people that we asked.

Time was pushing on as we searched the back roads for the address that had been given me. Then at last we spotted a house, miles from anywhere. It had to be the one as a coffin was just being carried out of it. I decided to drive past, but unknown to me a set of 'go and stop' boards were being operated just around the corner from the house. Sod's law decided to play a big part that day, the board was on stop, and it was only a few minutes before the hearse pulled up behind us. The next thing I remember was a chap in a black hat pushing a door key into my hand.

Then there was the time when we were asked to cater for a large function for a lord that was having a bit of a bash. The house was set in very large grounds and the gentleman in question had a butler that I had known for many years. As we set out the food and bottles of wine I thought that many bottles of wine were slowly disappearing. Then I noticed the butler going up and down the stairs every few minutes. It became clear that he wanted his own private wine stock because after a while he had removed twenty bottles of wine. After a little word in his master's shell-like we soon stopped that.

Over the 12 years we were often asked to cater for functions that would be attended by one or more of the royal family. A few weeks before the function I would have to go and see the royal protection officer at Dersingham, and give him a list of the staff that be working at the function. Within a few days he would ring me and say you can't bring her, or he can't come. The reasons for the refusal might relate to a silly little thing that happened ten years ago like riding their bikes with out lights, or maybe thumping some one in the face at the office party.

Catering for the Royals became second nature for us. It may have been that the function was when the Duke or Prince Charles was visiting a factory but in many cases it was in one of the grand houses of Norfolk.

On one occasion we were asked to cater for a party of around two hundred people and we were informed that H.R.H Princess Anne would be the VIP guest that evening. As luck would have it all my staff was passed ok by the protection police and we duly arrived at the house. We started to unload the van and it was then a police officer told me that once we had unloaded the van we were to move it to a marked out area that was almost a ten minute walk from the house. That was just in case we had a bomb on board I suppose.

As if that was not enough to contend with, as we entered the kitchen, that was our work place, we found it was full of police officers, and they all had guns. Then to my amazement I noticed more guns were lined up along one of the walls. It was then I asked a silly question that a burly police officer did not find funny. "If there's any trouble, Mr police officer, which gun is mine?"

Cooking at the house at Sandringham was one of the experiences that left a mark on my memory. We had to cook for the BBC film crew. The instructions were that we had to be at the house at four in the morning to cook breakfast for the thirty or so crew that were down here to film the Prince of Wales in connection with the Princes Trust.

As my motley crew and I drove into the estate under the cloak of darkness all was going well. Slowly my red van made its way towards the house and the kitchen door. Then from nowhere came an armed policeman, and then another and another. Very quickly in fact we were surrounded. " Please get out of the van and stand there. We want every thing out of the van please."

So we unloaded the van and the next thing that happened was a sniffer dog jumped in and started doing what sniffer dogs do best. As the dog made his exit from the van he made a beeline for one of the metal containers and started to bark. A dog barking in that way seemed like music to the royal protection police. They became very uneasy and one of them even slipped his gun from his shoulder. The dog continued to bark his head off at this box. "Open it up for us."

The word please was not used this time. The dog was called off as I slowly walked towards the box and lifted the lid. I was told to lift the contents out slowly at arms length. This I did and out came ten pounds of the finest pork sausages you could ever ask for.

We as a company, Colin Rushmore Cuisine, were involved in catering for small dinner parties, or catering for 1400 guests at a 21st birthday bash. Often arriving home in the wee small hours, as it was just getting light, only to start out again for another function. Maybe this time we were catering, in a field, for a seed company that was entertaining one hundred farmers. After the 12 years of loading and unloading the vans; driving miles to functions; catering in kitchens that you could not swing a cat around I decided that it was time to call it a day.

Outside catering must be one of the hardest parts of the trade to enter, but in its defence it has taken me into places that the general public will never have the chance to see. I once was employed by a gipsy to do his daughter's wedding. The gent in question became a loyal friend, as have many of the lords and ladies I catered for. It has left me with many happy memories of times and the people. Not forgetting the weird experiences that we had over the years that we were in the outside catering lark.

Heacham Village Sign

Rushmore's
The Restaurant

As we open the doors at Rushmore's ready for another dinner session, the car park begins to fill. It's time again to get the show on the road. It will not be long before some one will shout "Check on". That's the signal for me to turn up the heat, and soon the kitchen will be running at maximum speed.

With for now eight to ten orders on the check board and lots more to come: one smoked salmon with prawns and Cromer crab, two pancakes, two brown shrimp fishcakes with lemon butter, followed by two slow baked fillets of lamb, one salmon, one fillet steak filled with stilton cooked medium and one rabbit cooked in cider sauce, the pressure is heating up. This is the same pressure that's experienced in any kitchen in the land which is trying to provide freshly cooked cuisine for their customers.

As you start to pan fry fillets of sea bass, and turn down the heat on the hollandaise sauce to stop it splitting; the other six pans on the stove that contain food and dishes cooking in the ovens will all require your attention. It's a juggling act that you perform each night, often not always with the perfection that you would wish for and desire. But perfection is the name of the game. I have a saying that my commis chef could recite in his sleep, "preparation is better that perspiration".

The check board is now full, the heat is on. "Table two away, please." Or words to that affect and as the waitress takes the order out we are shouting "Table nine away. Come on you lot, food's going cold, and what about table ten? Have they finished their starters?"

Normally the dinner service will last for three hours, with very little let up. All hell will be let loose if a problem occurs at the height of service. Then, as if you couldn't wait to finish the dinner service, the last table's order is whisked away. It's over! At least it's all over for the kitchen staff that work on the stoves. It's time now for me to smarten myself up a bit and set foot into my restaurant to spend a little time chatting with the customers. Many of them are local, others come from further a field but all are most welcome.

Daniel, Colin, Cathy & Kim

Rushmore's restaurant is almost ready to celebrate its second anniversary. Looking back over the last two years it's probably time to take stock and reflect. The time has slipped by. I often wonder where it has gone as it seems as if it was only last week that we opened the doors for the first time. Yes, my customers tell me, I can cook, but one chef cannot run a restaurant on his own. It doesn't work unless you have, as I do, a small band of great hard working staff that it is a privilege to work with. Each person is in total command of their department, so offering my customers a friendly and professional service [thanks guys].

Now for me, as the Rushmore's restaurant heads for its second birthday, I in the next year will be saying goodbye to the fifties and hello to the sixties. Now I can hear you saying "How long can he go on for? I thought he was only around mid fifties. Pushing sixty cor blimey."
Well the answer is as long as I can. I fondly remember my dear old grandfather still riding his bike would you believe it, with a young lady on the cross bar, at the age of 82.

Heacham Village Green opposite the Church

Conclusion

People often tell me that they can remember things that happened fifty odd years ago, but can't remember what happened two days ago. Maybe like me it's a sign of getting old. As I started to write this book, rekindled memories came flooding back. My first day in the kitchen at the Dukes Head Hotel, all those years ago, is as clear in my mind as if it was only yesterday.

Working as a chef over these many years has not always been plain sailing. If I was asked to give advice to any young person that was thinking of becoming a chef then my answer would be, don't. Well not unless they can offer total commitment, and have a natural passion and love for food

With fond memories I remember my own mentor, Frank Cotton. He has always inspired me to help other young chefs. Those that have made it to the pinnacle of dizzy heights in the bright lights of London have given me a great sense of achievement in the knowledge that I played a small part in their career. But in each case I only offered them a step on the ladder. It was their determination, hard work, and very much their passion for food that drove them on to succeed.

I hope that through these pages I have given you an insight into the life of a Norfolk chef. At least now I won't have to worry in case my memory fails, as I shall always have my book of memories and tales to remind me of both the good and the bad times. Hopefully I have managed to produce the odd chuckle and inspired you to try a few of my recipes and of course if you are in the neighbourhood you can always pop in to my restaurant and say hello.